D1205002

SINS
OF THE
SOUTH

Big Secrets in a Small Town

by Maureen Hughes

Copyright, 2012 Maureen Hughes.

All rights reserved. No part of this book may be reproduced or utilized in any form or by any means, electronic or mechanical, including photocopying, recording or by any information storage or retrieval system without written permission of author.

Cover design by: Sara Ortiz (www.ortizdesignstudio.com)
Typesetting by: Sara Ortiz (www.ortizdesignstudio.com)
Cover and text photographs: courtesy of the author.
Printed in Danville, IL. United States of America

ISBN-13: 978-1469907796
ISBN-10: 1469907798
Library of Congress Control Number: 2012908076

Contact the author at:
maureen_3849@yahoo.com

I dedicate this book to Bob 'Butch' Winchester.

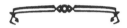

Once upon a time, a man walked upon the ground you now walk. He left footprints that held honor, respect, truth, and love during a fledging time in Illinois history. What better legacy can a father leave his son?

—Maureen Hughes

ACKNOWLEDGMENTS

Authors who have labored over the research in writing a book, which the subject matter is over 50 years old, know what I am referring to when I say there are limitations to information. Most of the material I received for this book came from the memories of people who lived in the area and time.

Many people in Cairo, IL and other small communities in and around Alexander and Pulaski counties showed me true southern hospitality while researching material for this book. The glasses of tart lemonade or ice tea were most refreshing as we sat in swings or front lawns under trees while stories were told to me. Much of the merit of this book goes to the forty-seven unnamed residents in and around Alexander and Pulaski counties who offered their time freely and information cautiously. They were helpful in the background of southern Illinois. I sensed they enjoyed returning to the era from their memories as I did listening to them, as my memory of Cairo didn't go that far back. To those wonderful people you have my heartfelt thanks for going out of your way to help me acquire the information needed. I, and those who read this account, am indebted to you for your truthfulness. I regret not being able to thank publically, by name, the many, many people who really made this a book. There were a few 'old time'

MAUREEN HUGHS

criminals that gave me background information on how certain rackets worked and who was in control of them. For obvious reasons they did not want to be identified. I have given partial identity of a person or two, at their request, to avoid hurting living family members.

Many of the stories caused a touch of jealousy to come over me. I wish I could hit the replay button and actually live in that time of history…if just for a while. Each of you has given me a valuable education and an endearing friendship.

Archie Slagle had the most detailed stories. Archie you were an angel! Some of his stories brought laughter, some brought tears as he remembered his old friend Lester 'Shot' Winchester. I truly wish Archie had lived long enough to see the story in print. I believed he would have thought justice served.

To Brett Berger my humble thanks for providing the pictures, articles, and written memories of your grandfather, Captain Elze Brantley of the Illinois State Police, districts 11 and 13.

To two public officials in Alexander County, my humble thanks to you for supporting my efforts and searching in dusty, moldy chambers for records long forgotten about. Some days the temperature was above 100 degrees as you faithfully worked with me. I cannot thank you by name at your request.

To the staff in the Records office of Pulaski County Court House who did their best to assist me in lowering heavy record books stacked too high. Lifting weights will be a resolution for me next year!

I saw honesty in the faces of the people that spoke candidly to me. I saw passion and concern as to how this crime could have happened. These are the people who have lived with the truth of what *really* happened *and* the fear of what would happen to them if they spoke up. More than five decades later they have spoken. I am deeply indebted to all of you.

Louise Ogg offered much to the early life in Cairo and the history of many of the buildings there.

I owe a huge thanks to Evelyn Lockard who is a walking encyclopedia for Pulaski County. A darling lady that added humor to her stories.

Linda Banks, historian for the Herrin City Library in Herrin, IL, told me the origins of the White Castle Nightclub, which was built by her grandfather on the south side of Herrin. The nightclub was robbed the same night that the Club Winchester was hit.

Others offered to contribute but decided against it. These people would not answer their phones or doorbells or keep appointments that *they* made to accommodate *their* schedules. People who *had* the authority to grant me the right to search for records delayed me with elementary excuses. These people have left me wondering if the open corruption that was evident in the 1940's and 1950's is not still going on today.

Closer to my heart a very special thanks to D&D. Love ya' bunches!

AUTHOR'S NOTE

Early summer of 2010, Robert Winchester, Illinois 19th Congressional District Republican State Committeeman contacted me to investigate the death of his father, Lester 'Shot' Winchester. My first true crime book, *The Countess and the Mob* had just been published and I was on the book-signing trail. He had read the book and wanted to discuss whether I would consider looking into a 50-year-old cold case. According to the inquest, Lester Winchester committed suicide in 1956 but the jury requested the state of Illinois to investigate further. This was *never* done, leaving Robert Winchester wondering if it was something else... like murder!

Within an hour I was intrigued enough about Lester Winchester to look into his case. I traveled to the southern tip of Illinois. Cairo, Illinois to be specific, to begin my investigation. Sifting through old, musty record books, searching libraries for newspaper articles on the case and talking to people who remember the details proved a challenge...even for a seasoned investigator. Records had been destroyed either by acts of God, carelessness, or, worse, intentionally. I found the people of Cairo and small neighboring towns genuinely warm and welcoming. Most were receptive until I asked if *they* thought Mr. Winchester's death was suicide. I was honest and open from the start but found walls of indifference concerning this case. I learned an entirely new meaning to 'the nature of evil' and the entrenchment of it in second and third generations of some residents.

For more than 50 years the death of Lester 'Shot' Winchester has remained the subject of conversation only to family members and close, close friends. For the same number of years suspicion has clouded the results of the inquest and the official death certificate. Until now. Officially ruled a suicide by an inquest jury, photos of the crime and those who remember what really happened told an entirely different story. Suicide is not a plausible explanation for Shot's death. Suicide is not committed without premeditation. Normally, there is sufficient evidence to support a *true* suicide.

The cause of death in the case of Lester 'Shot' Winchester was closed even though members on the jury requested the state of Illinois to investigate further due to ambiguous evidence. The truth about his death is webbed in a veil of secrecy known only to a few. I knew someone somewhere knew the true events of that April night in 1956. Finding the person or persons seemed impossible. Then I received the phone call I had been waiting for. I never saw the individual just listened to the raspy voice on the other end. He told me why Shot Winchester was killed. He told me why the testimony of people was trumped up and rehearsed. Why those giving testimony in court were pressured into lying under oath. The caller said he had heard rumors that one witness even received a 'gift' of a car several weeks after the inquest. The car was not new but new to him as he had never owned one that would run good. Why did this man, telling me this story fifty years after the fact not go to the authorities with what he knew? Because the local law enforcement was involved and the mobsters that controlled the local cops would be implicated and *he* would be dead for talking. His punishment was living with the truth all the years since. After we hung up I thought... small towns hide big secrets.

Most readers of mob-associated criminals are thinking of major cities like Las Vegas, New York or Chicago as the territory for notable criminals like Bonnano, Capone and Segal. Those cities and those criminals made national headlines. Journalists and reporters didn't identify the sub headlines from outside the corporate limits of these major metropolises. The media ignored the rural counties that were the target of the criminal elite. The group of mobsters that worked outside the big cities but held an equally deadly grip on the smaller towns, businesses, and people did not make headlines. Investigators have ignored these people. Their cases have been buried under piles of litigation or literally buried through payoffs to be forgotten about.

In *Sins of the South,* I have written the story as it was told to me through various people in various communities and states. They have explained how life was during and after prohibition and how Shot Winchester's death was set up and how those involved literally got away with murder. Knowing that there is no statue of limitation on murder explains the sudden silence of many of the people when questioned about this case. Ruled a suicide, Lester 'Shot' Winchester's death had been a politically correct way of saying *cover-up*. This is the way the South. The way it has *always* worked.

I hope within these pages the truth is apparent and the man everyone knew as 'Shot' can finally rest in peace.

Truth, like gold, is to be obtained not by its growth, but by washing away from it all that is not gold.

Leo Tolstoy

MAUREEN HUGHS

Prologue

Late evening on February 23, 1956, Alfred Leroy Reahm and Norman Halliday Jr. walked into the Tin Inn tavern north of Cairo, IL with guns. The two men sat at the bar and ordered drinks. Noticing that they were the only customers, Reahm decided to get down to the purpose of being there: robbing the owner. Hearing his dog bark ferociously owner Clate Adams entered the business part of the tavern to see what was causing the dog to bark. The dog was immediately shot to death and then so was Clate Adams.

At their trial, Reahm and Halliday were convicted of first-degree murder in the death of Clate Adams. Alfred Reahm, in an attempt to reduce his sentence, implicated Lester Winchester as being in on the murder. Bob Aldridge, County Sheriff of Olmsted, IL immediately requested a warrant for the arrest of Lester 'Shot' Winchester.

Early morning, April 7, 1956 nightclub owner, Shot Winchester, drove by *Club 37*, which he owned, for what would be his last time. Shot was to meet a friend who said he could help keep Shot from going to prison. The Pulaski county sheriff was looking for Shot to serve a warrant for his arrest for something he did not do. His new 1956 two-toned blue Oldsmobile was traveling on new Route 37 two miles south of Olmsted in Pulaski County in southern Illinois. Turning onto old Route 37 Shot drove slowly down the concrete road. Oak, maple, and ash trees cast eerie shadows on the road. Shot turned off his headlights and lit an unfiltered Camel cigarette as he crept down the winding road. He stopped just beyond a state highway maintenance driveway, backed into the drive, and with the car engine running, waited. Nothing. No one. Finishing the cigarette, he turned back north, drove to the edge of a thicket of trees, and waited. A few minutes later, he turned the car around in the road using the moonlight sifting through the trees to guide his way. He rolled the driver's window down to let the cool morning air in. He was nervous. Again, he slowed down at the highway maintenance driveway and looked around. Nothing, just the *click,click* of a few crickets coming out of hibernation and the steady hum of his car engine.

Headlights were coming from the north on the new Route 37 and then disappeared. He had to keep moving. Again turning north, he met a truck and slowly passed it. He sat there and waited a few minutes. Nothing. Making a u-turn in the road he, again, headed south. *Where was he?* He drove to the end of old Route 37, waited, and listened. Nothing. Turning around and heading back north, he drove to the entrance of old Route 37and sat there. No traffic whatsoever appeared. He would make one more pass south. He turned back south barely moving down

2

the road. Just north of the maintenance driveway, a few feet north of a sand pile Shot saw a figure of a man on his left, waving his arm. The man approached out of the trees. Shot stopped. It was Bill Harris his friend and part-time employee.

"What took you so long Bill?" Shot asked as he put the gearshift in park.

"Shot, I talked to Bob. They just want to talk to you… ask you a couple of questions…that's all." Bill Harris said as he leaned against the Oldsmobile.

"Bob wants more than that, Bill. He wants to hang this on *me*. He hates me enough to haul me in and…why are you shaking Bill?"

"Shot, they just want to *talk* to you."

"Who's *they* Bill? You keep saying they."

"You know. Bob and….

Bill Harris stood up straight and stepped away from the car as Jake Rubin approached the Oldsmobile. He stood there a moment with his hands in his coat pockets. Taking a step closer Rubin reached for the car door handle.

"Push over so we can talk Winchester. Get in the back Bill." Shot moved to the middle of the car as Jake Rubin got in the driver's seat and put his gloved hands on the steering wheel.

"Bob says we have a problem with this Reahms' thing. Bob thinks you will talk about some things to the Feds that he doesn't want out."

"I'm not saying a god damn thing. To you or anyone else."

"That's not the way Bob sees it. He's got too much to lose here. He can't take any chances if the Feds put pressure on you."

Looking past Rubin, Shot saw Bill Harris look out the passenger side of the car, curse and get out of the car. Rubin opened the driver's door and got out, slamming the door closed. Sensing something wasn't right Shot looked out the car's passenger window and saw a man's silhouette in the gray morning light standing on the shoulder of the road. His left hand hung to his side. His right hand held something against his leg.

Shot looked back at Harris standing on the shoulder of the road.

"What have you done Bill?" Shot knew then it was a set up.

Leaning into the car, Jake Rubin turned the radio on. "We have to solve this problem Shot…now. For everyone's sake. You should have played along Shot. You should have played along."

The thud of muffled bullets and the shattered glass on the passenger side was forever held within the rows of trees along old route 37.

Some two hours later Shot Winchester was wheeled into the emergency room at St. Mary's Hospital in Cairo barely clinging to life. Past the group of people and cops that had gathered and behind the stretcher that carried the mortally wounded Winchester, Sheriff Bob Aldrich hastily closed the emergency doors.

"We got him boys. We finally got the son of a bitch!"

The First Sin

JULY 16, 1913

Lester Winchester walked into the courtroom with lowered eyes and cuffed hands. He sat down at the defense table with the attorney appointed to him. He turned to scan the courtroom for his parents. When the judge took his seat and announced 'court in session', Lester Winchester would be asked to answer to the charge of murder with intent.

They are all watching me. Their eyes move from me to my mother. My hands are sweating as I laced my fingers together. My shirt cuffs are even moist from the sweat. My father sits stoic, with no expression on his face. Didn't they know that it is wrong to lie? That it is wrong to cheat a person. Even the Bible says so. I begged him to take it back. All of it. He said awful things about my mother. He doesn't even know my mother! He just didn't want to admit he cheated. I hate cheaters and I hate liars.

The jury looked at the young boy who sat with his head

down. The hair combed so neatly and the part so straight. The starched shirt and the scuffed high top boots couldn't belong to a killer.

"May I remind the jury that you are to weigh *all* the evidence and testimony that has been presented in this case. This young lad, Mr. Lester Winchester, is being tried for murder in the first degree. You must return a guilty verdict if the evidence presented here is beyond a reasonable doubt. If you have *reasonable* doubt that he committed murder then you must return a not guilty verdict. You are to remain in the jury room until you have reached a verdict. At that time, you will tell the bailiff that you are ready to return to the courtroom. Do you understand your task?" Instructed the judge.

"Yes, your honor. We do." Said the jury foreman. The other jurors nodded their heads yes. The trial of a young man, fifteen years old was ending. This was indeed an emotional situation for everyone involved. A murder in a small town in southern Illinois. A young man killing another young man over being cheated in a dice game. Bad in and of itself this was just the beginning for Lester Winchester.

Romancing Southern Illinois

The gateway to the South is not Louisville, Kentucky or Richmond, Virginia. It is not even Baton Rouge, Louisiana. At the southern tip of Illinois lay a town well-documented in books, movies, newspapers and even the war room in Washington D.C. Cairo, Illinois, a town in Alexander County, is the true gateway to the south. Pulaski, Union, Massac, Johnson, and Williamson are all counties in Illinois that are south of the Mason-Dixon Line. Cairo, Illinois, which is the most southern town in that state, was once a pivotal port city in American history with a rich heritage. The southern counties in Illinois that make up the gateway to the south have hung on to many old southern traditions: BBQ, lemonade, molasses, porch swings, and hollyhocks. The residents never gave up the slow speech, the southern dialect or southern manners and way of life.

There was a time when southerly influence was monumental in Cairo. Cairo's elite lived on Washington Avenue. Statuesque Victorian style homes with wrap-around porches graced the street; a perfect setting for afternoon teas with neighbors, celebrities, and politicians discussing national affairs over brandy and cigars. Eighty-foot magnolia trees bursting with six to eight inch white blossoms lined the brick streets. Honeysuckle hanging on picket fences greeted the dawn with an intoxicating scent that filled the residential sections.

Only the best artisans were summoned to Cairo to capture the Italian Renaissance and Queen Ann periods in the banks, churches, and hotels that graced the brick streets in the business district. These businesses provided the bustling activity that drew customers and sightseers from neighboring states. The Safford Library and the opera house offered knowledge and culture not usually found beyond the East coast. The ornate Gem Theater that seated close to 700 offered affordable entertainment in the latest movies. The Kennedy and Halliday hotels provided comfortable accommodations for weekend visitors. The levee, which gave Cairo its initial importance, gave young lovers a place to cast their wishes on falling stars as steamers and paddle boats made silky waves in the moonlight.

This splash of land called Cairo between two great rivers was to be the most memorable city, outside of the nation's capital, east of the Mississippi River. Its history going back to Lewis and Clark before settlement. In the days of the Civil War, the meshing of the Ohio and Mississippi Rivers brought industry by the score that supported an abundant labor force. However, the town carried the stigma of being scandal-ridden and very deadly. Its penchant for crime has remained throughout its history.

The city thrived until the end of the Civil War. Post-Civil War left Cairo struggling to regain its strength for years afterwards. Former slaves and homeless southerners and immigrants came to Cairo to start a new life. They were risk takers; *all* of them for one reason or another. They set out to start a new life, risking everything they had. They were profiled and segregated. They took the most demeaning jobs just to eat and clothe their children. They accepted less pay than the established citizens of Cairo. However, they kept their values and traditions. This influx of new people put a financial and social strain on the town. Cairo did not welcome the droves of people who were entering the city and this melting pot of nationalities and colors began to simmer.

Along with the immigrants and misplaced war survivors came the criminal element. Thieves, swindlers, and prostitutes made up the largest part of this element. Many of the new settlers were former inmates of area prisons and penitentiaries. Prostitutes, which numbered in the hundreds, supported three bordellos on one street. The hooligans had it made in Cairo and they knew it. Too much ill gotten money filtered through the town and no town official was going to stop it.

Any downtrodden area of the country is prime territory for gangsters to take control and Cairo was a hotbed of crime. Pirates, gamblers, and prostitutes had flourished since Cairo's infancy and it sure was not going to cease. Bars, dance halls, hotels, and gambling houses kept the silver coins and greenbacks in constant circulation. It was not long before Cairo, Illinois was dubbed 'one of the most wicked places in America.'

In spite of the ever-growing criminal element in the 20's and 30's, Cairo was *the* place to shop. Trolleys and ferries brought customers from Paducah, Kentucky to the Olmsted, Illinois landing in Pulaski County. From there they took public transportation on to Cairo. Big named stores graced the business district streets and business boomed for the river town.

However, Cairo was still a breeding ground for crime and in 1937 had the highest murder rate in the state of Illinois. Prostitution ranked as high as bootlegging. With the brothels next door to one another, it was easy for the town's street commissioner, Homer McDaniel, to collect the sin tax from the madams. Because of the tax, streets in Cairo were listed as the best-maintained streets in the U.S. Madams were charged $10.00 a week to keep their brothels and $5.00-$7.00 for each prostitute depending on their worth. Sometimes the brothel madam wasn't willing to pay the tax and would tell McDaniel that business had been bad that week. When McDaniel threatened to shut a brothel down, she would tell him that she had more control over his men than he did and would have his street dug up if he even thought about shutting her down! No further argument needed. With the onset of WWII, crime gripped the area and Cairo became a breeding ground for those who chose greed and quick money to become famous through self-imposed policies and rules.

Post WWII offered Cairo a growing population once again. Farmers who lost their farms during the war moved to town and started businesses. Others sold wedding rings and family heirlooms to pay taxes or make delinquent land payments and continued as farmers.

Industries were booming as a steady stream of boats and barges moved coal, cotton, sugar, and lumber to waiting trucks along Commercial Street which then transported the goods across the nation. Industrial employment was high in Alexander County and people in the neighboring states of Kentucky, Missouri, and Indiana found good jobs and wages here in Cairo.

To people in the northern part of Illinois southern Illinois became known as 'Little Egypt'. The biblical names for counties and towns within the counties gave neighboring states and municipalities a warm fuzzy feeling when talking about Cairo, Illinois. Nothing could have been further from the truth.

Rules of the South

The idea of a formal education in southern Illinois, as in many southern states in the early 1900's, was thought to serve as a source of dangerous ideas - too much so for young minds; higher education was not recommended for the children. Because of the influx of immigrants, displaced post-war people and blacks searching for a better life, most young adults in Cairo did not have social status, which left them somewhat displaced in society. Parents in these groups felt that sons should follow in their father's trade and an educated young woman reduced her chance of marriage. However, earning some form of living was a necessity. Many did choose to follow in the steps of their parents. There was no shame in hard work even if the pay was not great. Others sought easier ways of financial gain and a way to achieve it with the least amount of labor.

Bootlegging and rum running were, initially, the major occupation during the 1930's and easily into the 40's in the southern counties of Illinois. The end of Prohibition in 1933 didn't stop the bootlegging. It merely meant that they could continue with their business of smuggling illicit booze tax-free. Those who made the moonshine did so to supplement their meager incomes and sometimes serve as their *only* income during the Great Depression and other slow economic periods. Those involved in rum running were socially looked down upon but felt that this and other vices would make them wealthier than those breaking their backs at hard labor with little gain. Cockfights in the backwoods provided entertainment while the mash simmered in the copper stills.

Most of the southern Illinois gangster CEOs concentrated on the booze business. They were not involved in the making of moonshine due to the risk of being discovered by revenuers. Shipping it, distributing it, and protecting it, on the other hand, was a lot safer. They knew the liquor business came with a profit guarantee. The sultans of Alexander County and other counties in southern Illinois were blisters on society as a whole. Most never made an honest living and instead crushed the life out of many local businesses. And in some cases the life of the business owner.

If the need for businesses and income is prevalent among the people then the infiltration of gangsters becomes the source of new entrepreneurs in that area. Territory was essential for gangsters to survive and gain power. The more territory they could acquire the more power they had. Profits from their illegal businesses gave them the needed power to control not only the residents of a town but also law enforcement officials and politicians. Owning cops and politicians meant securing their powerful alliance with the government.

The counties in southern Illinois that made up Little Egypt were prime territory for the sucking tentacles of the ambitious crime leaders in the St. Louis, Chicago, and Memphis areas in the 1930's and 1940's. For southern Illinois, the criminal rogues were as thick as the cowboy was in the Wild West. But there were honest, hardworking people too.

Among the settlers in Johnson County was Robert C. Winchester. Growing up in Virginia, Robert did what most young did when the War Between the States broke out. He joined up. Though records are sketchy, it is believed he was an officer and served the Union side during the Civil War. Familiar with the area Robert was in charge of transporting iron ore from Elizabethtown, Illinois to the naval yard in Mounds City, Illinois. Located on the Ohio River the town was the base for U.S. Grant's army prior to the invasion of the south. Mounds City was the only Union shipyard for the North and maintained an average of 80 vessels including seven ironclad gunboats.

Settling down in Vienna, IL, the Winchesters' raised two sons, Ernest and Lester and two daughters, Bernard and Anna Mae. The children attended elementary school in New Burnside, Illinois and high school in Vienna, Illinois. New Burnside, a small community, didn't offer much for young people so they ventured to the nearby town of Vienna, Illinois to find work and entertainment. Like other small communities, it was customary in the area to nickname sons.

Ernest became 'Big Shot' to locals and Lester, idolizing his big brother, became 'Little Shot'. By his late teens, Lester was just called Shot Winchester by almost everyone. As young men, the brothers invested in taverns and a pool hall in Vienna. Ernest's tavern was near the town's square. Lester had a flower shop in town and the Curve Inn tavern west of Vienna. Lester took his profits from the tavern business and invested in land. At an early age, Lester had lofty plans of one day owning his own classy nightclub.

Shot Winchester grew up working at any job he could he could find. He had plans and goals he was determined to make real. An incident when Lester was 15 years old set those dreams back several years. A friendly dice game after school with schoolboys turned deadly when a school chum cheated Shot out of his money. Martin W. of Carbondale, Illinois tells the story as it was told to him by the son of one of the players.

"Shot caught the boy using 'loaded' dice on some of the throws and asked for the money he had lost when the loaded dice was used. The boy denied having another pair and a struggle broke out when Lester reached for the boy's pant cuff. Shot had seen him replace the regular dice with the loaded dice hidden there. The boy started calling Shot names and then called Shot's mother a foul name. Shot asked him to take it back, return his money and all would be forgiven. The boy refused and continued to refer to Shot's mother as a bitch and other foul names. The other boys in the game tried to get him to return the money to Shot but instead the boy got louder and more vulgar insulting Shot's entire family. He remained calm and asked, once again, for his money back and an apology. If the friend would do that all would be forgotten. But, the friend, too embarrassed by then to do that in front of the other boys turned and went back to the dice game.

Once home Shot went to the closet grabbed the shotgun and returned to the sight of the dice game. Once again, he asked the friend to take back the insults towards his family. Once again, the friend refused. Shot raised the shotgun and fired it into the chest of the friend killing him."

Returning home, Shot changed clothes and placed his tie-up shoes neatly in the closet in his room. He placed the gun in the closet off the parlor and took his place at the supper table saying nothing about the incident. Shortly after supper, the sheriff came to the Winchester home to questioned Shot and his family. Shot would only say he had just come home from school. The police, not satisfied began to search the house for the gun. While the sheriff searched for the gun, another officer found the neatly placed shoes in Shot's closet. Picking up the shoes, the cop could see blood splatters on the toes of both shoes. He brought the shoes out and showed the sheriff who then placed Lester under arrest for suspicion of murder.

On July 15, 1913, Lester 'Shot' Winchester was found guilty of murder and sentenced to serve 36 years at the Menard Correctional Center in Menard, Illinois. This was a shock to his mother as Shot was a juvenile but due to the charge of intent to commit murder he was on his way to the roughest penitentiary in the state of Illinois at the tender age of 15.

Shot proved to be a model prisoner and the warden showed favor with him. Once a month, Warden J. B. Smith, took Shot home to see his family in Vienna. While serving his time Shot became interested in horticulture and was granted the sole responsibility of maintaining the grounds around the prison. He convinced the warden to plant shrubs, trees, and new varieties of flowers and ground covers. Being a trusted prisoner, Shot was given the responsibility of landscaping the Deputy Warden's home along with the prison yards. He also convinced Warden Smith to construct a green house where he and others could grow their own plants for the prison yards; Shot's love for flowers stayed with him long after his release.

During Shot's incarceration, the government sponsored a medical experiment. The purpose of the tests were to see what medications worked to control or alleviate malaria and symptoms of the disease. Shot did not suffer from the disease but learned that volunteering to test the medications would reduce his sentence. Little was known or recorded about the side effects of the medication. For Shot Winchester it meant losing most of his hair.

On August 4, 1922, Shot Winchester was paroled from Menard penitentiary. His dream of having a nightclub still lingered in his head while he held odd jobs for locals and stashed as much of his pay away as he could for the next two years. On August 4, 1924, Lester Winchester was formally discharged from the Menard penal system.

Knowing that he needed big money for the nightclub he dreamed about Shot ran moonshine from a local still to Paducah and Murray, Kentucky, using back roads in hopes of avoiding the Feds. He used a borrowed truck and shared his earnings with the owner of the truck. He only had one narrow escape with the revenuers.

It was routine for Shot to place the containers of illegal booze in the back of the truck bed and cover the cases with a tarp. He then piled livestock manure on top of the tarp disguising the illegal booze. Late one night, revenuers stopped Shot and asked where he was going. Shot stated that he had stayed too long at his girlfriend's and needed to unload the manure before he returned home. Finding the odor disgusting the revenuers didn't even walk to the back of the truck and waved him on. Grinning, Shot proceeded to his destination.

Southern Illinois wasn't far behind the big cities when it came to structured outlaws. The Shelton gang, notorious and well infiltrated, in southern Illinois, had used young Shot Winchester to make bootleg runs for them. As an occasional employee, he ran a route to Vienna, Harrisburg, Elizabethtown, Thebes, and Golconda (all in Illinois). Shot didn't know the Sheltons as history portrays them but rather as an occasional paycheck. He didn't work with them directly but through another man employed by Carl Shelton. The Shelton brothers preyed on Shot's inexperience and only paid half of what they paid an experienced driver to run the whiskey, rum, and moonshine. When the owner of the truck found out he was working for the Shelton's the rent on the truck went up. Nevertheless, Shot was happy with the $400-$500.00 dollars a week he made. Having a good head for business, Shot saved at least half of what he made trucking booze, and hid it in various places. He still held to the dream of owning a nightclub someday. He knew it would be years before he could save enough to accomplish this but he also knew tucking away a few hundred dollars here and there would eventually grant him his wish.

Major rumrunners had longer routes and faster cars and trucks than Shot Winchester. The drivers would be gone for 4 or 5 days barring vehicle trouble. If they had the northern route, they went to Danville, Kankakee, Chicago, and the Chicago suburbs in Illinois. The southern route went to Missouri, Florida, Alabama, Mississippi, and Louisiana. A five-day pay was close to $2,000.00 for the runners. It was a two-man job non-stop to the destination. Taking all the back roads to their destination one man drove while the other man slept.

The Volstead Act, passed in 1919, enabled the government to enforce the 18th Amendment. Manufacturing, transporting, selling, or trading liquor carried stiff penalties and fines. Andrew Volstead and his Act meant to benefit society as a whole, but crime, gangs and lawlessness rose to new heights in America because of it. The ringleaders of crime called themselves *Mafia*.

It didn't take the Mafia long to see a wide open door to enter during Prohibition. The prominence of the mafia in America can be blamed on prohibition. They saw that the American people were not going to stop consuming alcohol just because a law passed stating no more alcohol in America. The East coast mobsters began the trail of organized crime that quickly spread across the United States through the enactment of Amendment 18 and the Volstead Act. It also allowed organized crime to achieve power and influence well into the 1970's.

Al Capone, who took the reins in leading the mobsters of Chicago, didn't miss a beat in seeing the profits of illegal booze. He knew southern Illinois was economically depressed during the 1920's, 1930's, and 1940's and ripe for the underworld to capitalize on satisfying the thirst in southern Illinois. Capone was well aware of the Shelton and Birger gangs and their power in southern Illinois. In an attempt to gain a piece of the action Capone and five body guards met representatives of the Shelton gang in Effingham, Illinois to discuss a territorial plan where everyone could be happy and financially healthy. Capone soon learned the power that the Shelton gang had in southern Illinois and out of respect decided to leave the southern section of the state to them. Well, that was the impression he left with the Sheltons.

Capone wasn't going let a financial opportunity the entire lower third of a state could produce pass him by. He never dealt with the Shelton or the Charlie Birger gangs head on. He knew it wasn't worth it. However, by coming around from the East and the West he could grab a portion of the state's income from bootlegging. He had friends in Terre Haute and Evansville, Indiana. Besides, northern Indiana had become the Outfit's own 'unmarked cemetery'.

Several business and political contacts in Springfield, Illinois and St. Louis, Missouri would bring information to him. He used these friends and contacts to make the necessary business dealings to acquire a portion of the bootleg business. Capone's territory was elastic and stretched to the levees of Cairo, Illinois. His plan of owning Illinois was taking shape.

During prohibition, Shot gained employment at Paul Miller's Dairy in Vienna. Trucks from Metropolis delivered containers labeled 'milk' from local dairy farms in 5-gallon containers. In reality, beer and whiskey were in the containers, which were then carried to the back of the dairy's processing plant. Most of the truck's cargo was stolen or highjacked from other trucks. The stolen booze was brought to Metropolis and reloaded onto different trucks with 'Dairy' signs on the sides. Once at Miller's Diary the beer and whiskey was relabeled and delivered in different 5-gallon milk jugs to local taverns, hotels, and private residences by Shot. No one was the wiser and for Shot Winchester it was a way to fulfill his dream.

While working in legal jobs where he could, Shot continued to run booze when called upon. Finding him trustworthy, local gangsters entrusted him with an occasional southern route, which involved the 'dry' southern states. A case of Canadian Club cost the runners $30 to $35. The delivery netted them up to $500. In Illinois and southern Missouri. In Mississippi, Georgia and Louisiana the cost skyrocketed to $1,500. Making more deliveries and expanding his routes, Shot became aware of men who had earned a reputation with the criminal element in Alexander County; men you avoided in public and paid respect to in private. George and Art Garner, The Purple Gang, Jake Rubin, Mary and Ely Sergent, Ben Fishel, and the notorious Frank 'Buster' Wortman. These people were the sultans of Little Egypt's Alexander and Pulaski counties.

The Sultans of Southern Illinois

In the early 20th century, the town of Cairo, Illinois was producing noticeable statistics. The town had the highest arrest rate and by the mid 1930's the highest murder rate. Chicago couldn't compete in the stats. Several criminal entrepreneurs were setting stakes in Alexander and Pulaski Counties.

In southern and southwest Illinois short, unassuming Frank 'Buster' Wortman was king. His main job, initially, was to keep the Chicago mafia family out of East St. Louis. Wortman was well known by the mafia due to his high interest in the numbers racket in Brooklyn, New York. Buster's first taste of crime occurred while serving under Carl and Bernie Shelton several miles southeast of East St. Louis.

The Sheltons were well entrenched in prostitution, gambling and bootlegging in the East St. Louis area shortly after Prohibition was enacted. Buster, at age 21, was jack-of-all-trades and willing to do anything. When not in prison he worked for a steel casting plant, flirted in politics for a legal income, and did jobs for the Sheltons. In the late 1920's Wortman was guarding a moonshine still owned by the Sheltons when a Prohibition agent, acting on a tip, discovered the hidden still. Wortman, prone to a quick temper, beat him severely but not bad enough that the agent couldn't identify who did the beating. Tried and convicted, Buster Wortman was given ten years at Leavenworth Federal Penitentiary. Not a country club for criminals, Leavenworth held the worst of the worst criminals and became Buster's conduit to other high profile gangsters from around the country.

While serving his term he found favor with Murray Humphrey of the Chicago Outfit who was also serving time. Murray Humphrey's biggest business was laundering money. He bought two laundry businesses. One he kept legitimate to throw off cops, investigators, and federal agents. The second served to launder extortion money from downstate Illinois and the St. Louis area. Proceeds were then divided between Capone, whom Humphrey worked for, the Springfield, Illinois mob connections and himself.

By 1931, Murray Humphrey's money laundering racket netted the mob $50 million. Wortman and Humphrey formed an alliance against the Shelton gang and Buster Wortman vowed that if Capone would grant him the southern Illinois territory he would topple the Shelton gang. In agreeing to this, Capone's plan to infiltrate the southern counties of Illinois was working. Springfield, Illinois was already in his pocket and to have bootleg money coming in from the lower third of the state made Illinois *his*.

Truck hijacking was another profitable business for gangs in southern Illinois. Liquor, cigarettes, furs, and stolen produce topped the list of items in demand. Shot Winchester was well aware of the hijacking that occurred along the levees in Cairo and Routes 3 and 51 into Cape Girardeau, Missouri. He avoided them when running his liquor but knew whom the kingpins behind the hijacking were and where they were going with the stolen goods. If he had contact with any 'route watchers' he displayed an uncanny ability to talk his way out of being robbed, beaten or worse.

Alexander County, being a melting pot for strangers, was not conscious of another group of hoodlums staking a claim to the profits of illegal ventures. The Bernstein brothers from Detroit, Michigan had earned a reputation in the protection business. Narcotics ran freely within the city limits of Detroit, as did extortion.

The Purple gang acquired its name from Detroit shopkeepers who had been robbed by the Bernstein brothers enough times to be referred to as 'purple' as in the color of rotten meat. Russian Jewish immigrants, The Bernstein brothers were shrewd in their business dealings and often brutal. Consisting of only relatives and a few close friends, the gang was very small in comparison to the Shelton gang, the St. Louis mobsters, and the Chicago Outfit. Somewhat loosely knit, the brothers did well in hijacking Canadian liquor at sites along the Detroit River and re-selling it watered down and under a different label in Ohio. Stolen bootleg netted millions for the gang but that wasn't their only enterprise. Dabbling in narcotics, the Purple Gang peddled dope to poor Detroit blacks. Raided many times by police on suspicion of holding drugs in their homes, the Purple Gang hid their drugs in purchased lots in and around Detroit and even a boathouse on Burt Lake.

However, like many of the mobsters in the 1920's and 1930's, their greed caused them to venture out into newer territories. They were well aware of the rum running in Memphis, Kentucky, Evansville, Indiana and across southern Illinois. Brothers Abe, Raymond, and Joe Bernstein decided to tap into the lucrative business causing problems for Buster Wortman and his men who had the hijacking routes sealed up for themselves. Or, so Wortman thought.

Coming into Illinois through Evansville, Indiana the Purple Gang had already plundered the gangs in Indiana, robbing and brutally beating or murdering the drivers of trucks running the routes to Elizabethtown and Marion, Illinois. Customers waiting on a delivery sent men out looking for the trucks. Finding badly beaten drivers along the road or dead in the ditches and empty trucks aroused the attention of Prohibition Agents. Men searching for their delivery of hijacked liquor had to play dumb if questioned by the agents and return home with nothing.

Through their short time of terror, the Purple gang succeeded in eluding law enforcement. Had the Purple gang concentrated on their business dealings in Detroit the bigger mobsters from the East coast would have had a much harder time getting their foot in the door. Nevertheless, greed and friction within the gang *and* the fact that they had no hard structure caused their demise leaving stronger, better-structured mobsters to overtake Detroit. The gang became history when one member turned state's evidence against other members, which led to murder convictions and lengthy prison sentences. One member who managed to stay immune from prosecution was Peter Licavoli. He took the remaining Purple gang associates, regrouped, and offered their services to St. Louis mobster Joseph Zerilli during the last few years of prohibition.

Zerilli had an interesting position with the mafia. He was a former member of the Purple Gang and served as crime boss in Detroit during the 1940's and early 1950's. He also held a lot of behind-the-scenes power in St. Louis, Missouri.

Southern Illinois had their share of gangsters besides the Sheltons and Birgers. Like many minor hoodlums, George and Art Garner were craps and poker dealers in back rooms of businesses and taverns. Residing in southeast Missouri, the wannabe criminals sought a more lucrative employment with Buster Wortman. The brothers idolized the picaresque life of Wortman and the action they had heard about. They wanted their ties and authority to come directly from Buster Wortman.

Buster took them on instilling in them the thought that viciousness in getting what they wanted would be necessary. *That* wasn't going to be a problem! Hijacking trucks carrying liquor and goods became a steady income for the Garners. Together or with a Wortman soldier, they would hijack trucks carrying the valued Canadian liquor, take it to stills in Missouri and southern Illinois, mix it with inferior booze, and sell it at top quality prices to local taverns, nightclubs, and stores at a handsome profit. Starting as low echelon gangsters the Garners wanted to advance in the ranks of Wortman's gang. To accomplish this they entered into extortion and murder doing well in both positions.

The sultans of Alexander County knew that crime *did* pay and political positions *were* won with money. Wortman bought the politicians from the bottom all the way to the top. He became a master at the game and exercised it if it served his needs. Little Egypt was filling up with criminals and those that were established as such were making new ones out of legitimate business owners.

Extortion wasn't a new form of control but not well publicized or used in southern Illinois. The Garner brothers changed this and earned much of their power through extortion. It was a straightforward crime and George did very well at it. George was not a team player at heart. He was out for himself and more than happy to fulfill a 'contract' on somebody. Together the brothers became piranhas in the protection racket. Art and George accepted payoffs from businesses and taverns in the southern counties for their so-called 'protection' against law enforcement and any businessmen who wanted a cut of illegal business that was going on within the legal business. Hired first by Buster Wortman to hijack trucks the Garners became a respected team in the arson-for-hire business. If businesses would not fork over payments for George and Art's protection, the owners were told "something bad could happen to their establishment." This was often termed as a 'free pass' meaning a warning to the business owner. Usually, this threat awarded the Garners the payoffs that were divided with Wortman in Cape Girardeau who then sent a percentage on to Capone in Chicago. Some owners were stubborn or would not consent to the devious acts of the

28

Garners and after a profitable weekend the tavern would be found totally wrecked or in ashes Monday morning. The message became *perfectly* clear.

Neither the Garners nor Buster Wortman restricted their control to just business owners. Wortman knew if he had the unions under his thumb, he would have control of the money. Wortman tapped into the big unions and the Garners hit on the smaller unions.

Arnold Rothstein, head of organized crime in the garment district of New York in the 1920's saw the lucrative possibilities of labor racketeering. The garment district kept a steady stream of immigrants employed. He would charge the employees up to one penny for each piece they cut or stitched together. Being English-illiterate and gullible, workers paid Rothstein out of their wages. After Rothstein's murder in 1928, Jacob Shapiro took over advancing the criminal influence to the designer firms, the truckers unions, and employment agencies for the same price. George Garner and Jake Rubin were all too eager to assist in distributing garments that had been hijacked from the East coast districts.

Like most gangsters, George Garner looked for ways he could profit without sharing with his boss. He left much of the 'gun for hire' contracts to his brother Art and dealt successfully in arson, extortion, racketeering, and hijacking.

The popularity of vending machines in the cities gave Wortman new ideas for ventures as he saw a huge financial market for vending machines in communities around the cities and small towns. He invested heavily in various coin-operated machines from the Ace Novelty Company and ABC coin machine companies. Frank's brother Ted was on the business deed but Frank took most of the money to fund his illegal businesses. He had trucks hauling his vending machines day and night into Alexander, Pulaski, Johnson, and other southern Illinois counties. His work gave him the monopoly on vending machines in southern Illinois and eastern Missouri. Stick gum, stamps, and gumballs were the most popular until in the 1930's when Glascocks Brothers in Muncie, Indiana, manufactured the first chilled bottled soda machines.

The machine was nothing more than an adaptation of the cigarette vending machine but bore big profits for Buster. Pennies and nickels provided Wortman with thousands of dollars annually in revenue when collected on a weekly or monthly basis by his 'collector' George Garner. Add that to the hijacked trucks carrying whiskey and cigarettes, and bottled soda the Gardner brothers, Wortman and Capone made out very well in southern Illinois.

Vending machines initially meant big revenue on the East coast. Mobsters filtered the business to the western and southern states under the control of the major mob families. A distributor would sell his machines to a specific operator in a specific area or route. Wortman, already having liquor hijacking and protection territory established, had no problem placing vending machines in his territory. The popularity of coin-operated machines had grown rapidly across the country and proved to be a huge moneymaker for Wortman and his soldiers. *Everybody* wanted this new form of revenue. Vending machines were in restaurants, nightclubs, taverns, and some stores. Wortman took over the distribution of them across Missouri and 'Little Egypt'. The revenue in horse parlors, crap games, and card games couldn't compare to the income he accumulated from the vending machine enterprises he had established. Low-level soldiers under the leadership of Wortman would service the machines, which provided a vital source of funds to finance criminal activities or launder their criminally obtained money. Being a cash-only business made it easy to skim off profits before taxes. Little or no paperwork was involved.

Any business owner wanting to put new or different vending machines in had to have the 'ok' from Wortman. If the business owner obtained a machine that wasn't Wortman's or installed it without 'permission' from Wortman, George Garner would be told to 'visit' the owner and explain how the system worked and who made the rules. If the business owner knew what was good for his business he *followed* the rules. Using fear and intimidation Wortman and the Garner brothers secured their power in the business. Both brothers served as the muscle for Wortman in the machine business. Again, it was George Garner the 'bagman' who showed up at the various businesses that had vending machines to collect the boss's share of the proceeds from the machines. In most cases, the cut was 60% to the owner of the machine and 40% to the business owner.

The pinball machine and the jukebox became the rage country-wide in the 1930's. Flashing lights, strange sounds and little steel balls running around the colorful board drew men and boys to challenge their skills. They were innocent enough looking games but designed to take the players money. Machines lined the walls in taverns and stuck in corners of storerooms in businesses. Stolen booze, cigarettes, and furs were bringing in $12 million a year but the pinball and jukebox industry meant even more. It was the latest moneymaker and *another* means to launder money for the mob. Seeing the booty the mob was making prompted the hoodlums of Alexander and Pulaski counties to figure out how to get their cut.

Wortman had worked a deal with Chicago and St. Louis companies that sold the machines and *encouraged* business owners to purchase from his vending machine retail outlet. Wortman controlled the pinball empire when it was just a game of chance and small prizes were offered. After the 'flipper' was added to the machines, it became a game of skill to entice teenage boys and men to compete.

If a rival company supplied the pinball machines, Wortman would hire George Garner or Jake Rubin to warn the owner of the infraction and suggest they re-think from whom they would buy pinball machines. If the business owner did not comply then Garner would give them a 'free pass' or warning. Wortman trained his soldiers to limit the warnings to two. On the second warning George would bust the establishment up. If the message still wasn't clear, Art Garner would be summoned to take the business owner out. Point made. Collections from the machines were done weekly in Cairo and surrounding towns. Saturday night 'collections' was the usual and most profitable for the mob. Collecting the money was referred to as a form of 'protection' or an insurance policy. Several were involved in the breakdown of the protection money. First the mobster, then the county lawyers and local cops, finally the politicians and judges. The complicity of the Cairo police and Alexander's county officers were no exception.

Many of the area business owners financed their business with loans from Frank Wortman. Banks were still getting on their feet after the war and cautious about lending money. If the local bank refused a loan, the entrepreneur would seek out Wortman for the money. Most of these loans were not on paper and collecting the interest was done on a weekly basis. This seemed workable for the borrower but what he was not told was the interest on that loan was calculated daily and couldn't be paid in portions but in full. Missing an interest payment guaranteed a warning. Two missed payments meant an unwanted visit by George Garner. Maybe the business was vandalized. Maybe the owner's vehicle was blown up. Whatever means necessary was used to get the attention of the person to pay on time. The 'collectors' would inflict whatever level of injury necessary to achieve what they wanted; which in the end was money. If the business owner continued to be late with the interest payment, he was not granted another 'free pass'. It was the end of the line for him.

When Buster Wortman wanted someone's vending machine territory, it was the smart thing to turn it over to him for the price he offered. Those that wanted to bid the territory out lost in every case. There was no discussion concerning vending machine territory. No offers to haggle over. If the territory wasn't given to Wortman a strict message was given. Leaving a body in a car or a truck sent a message that *everybody* understood. It was a non-verbal warning to others that when you refuse to give up your vending territory this is what happens to you. No money taken, no jewelry removed from your body...just a direct and *permanent* example.

The judicial system in southern Illinois worked somewhat differently than other places. For a killing due to not following the rules set by the mobsters, no investigation was forthcoming. At least, not a legitimate one. The cases would remain unsolved if the body was even found. To the loan sharks it was considered an even trade. If Buster Wortman was doing his own dirty work, he didn't have to threaten someone or destroy property. If he were questioned about his bookmaking operation he would deny having any part of it. "That's for criminals, not a business man like me." He would say. Those who understood how bookmaking was done also knew that it was controlled by the mafia. Wortman had the protection of The Outfit so denial was part of his game. All the bookmakers were either controlled by a crime syndicate or intimidated into paying a service fee. Under the Chicago Outfit's umbrella, Wortman just had to give 'the look' and the person would sell his family to pay up.

Michael T. of East St. Louis said of Frank Wortman, "Wortman didn't have any of the head Mafioso backing him. He had friends, a few cops in his pocket and a few mafia capos who he did business with help him out when needed. Sometimes they would hide him somewhere if federal agents were on his back about some crime that had been committed. He wasn't a 'made man' but someone who worked under the leadership of the Chicago syndicate."

Frank 'Buster' Wortman had one person to pacify between himself and Al Capone. Frank Zito. Zito was the most powerful downstate underworld figure. He was the godfather of Springfield, Illinois running the prostitution, gambling, and illegal liquor businesses. Zito's payoffs to cops, prosecutors, and politicians were close to $10,000 a week. Both gangsters served time together at Leavenworth. Wortman would talk about Zito and his power in a positive tone with other gangsters but secretly Wortman hated him. Buster knew Zito could have him wiped out with a nod of his head. Buster's power was secure in East St. Louis and taking over Zito's territory wasn't on the table. Zito knew that Wortman was more familiar with western and southern Illinois than he was so it was only good business to make Wortman responsible for the illegal gambling, prostitution and the other rackets in those areas. *He* could stay in the city and collect his booty from the rural areas through Frank Wortman.

Buster Wortman had one other occupation he left off his resume and failed to include in his tax returns. Al Capone controlled the Continental Press Service from Chicago to Florida. Pioneer News was a subsidiary of Continental and more localized in southern Illinois and St. Louis. Wortman provided Capone with muscle in controlling Pioneer News who illegally supplied race results to the tune of $20 million in bets annually. He had strong connections with Continental because the son of Bev Brown, a major stockholder in Continental, worked for Buster as a mechanic in the coin machine business.

In making a rum run to Anna, or Jonesboro Shot Winchester would pick up the betting slips from bookies in Johnson, Pulaski and Alexander counties and take them to a 'pick up' house or business to be taken on to Buster Wortman. Buster would have Capone's percentage delivered to Zito who would take *his* predetermined cut and the balance sent on to Capone. A soldier for Wortman would then give Shot his cut. Shot was doing well for himself. He kept to himself and continued to make money doing whatever was asked of him. He didn't socialize with any of Wortman's men nor hang out in bars and mingle with the Garners at the various clubs. In his dreams, he made the drawings of the nightclub he would one day build. Every penny not having a purpose saved for the day his dream could become a reality.

Not Mr. Personality, George Garner was an off and on regular at various nightspots in Alexander and Pulaski counties. A loner, George would seek out the nightclubs hierarchy and study their habits, their friends, and customers. Always in black, George was easy to spot on streets but not in clubs. Black slacks, shoes, jacket and hat and a navy blue shirt, George blended in, in the darkened clubs. Those who knew him socially called him a sociopath. Preferring to sit alone in a club, he drank alone saying nothing to anyone, not even the bartender. He would stare at customers as if memorizing their faces as he nursed his drink. No one would remember him entering the club *or* leaving it. Those who knew him intimately referred to him as a psycho. Emotionally unstable, George had a violent temper. It was a rule of thumb to avoid making eye contact with him for any length of time. He showed no emotion when wasting a person. Ordered to make a hit Garner would shadow his victim for the perfect time and place to fulfill the contract. Other times he could care less who was around to be a witness. *Nobody* was going to admit seeing George Garner kill someone.

Garner proved to be a staunch pimp for the girls he kept at the various clubs in which he held a financial interest. They were 'on call' 24/7 minus a week off once a month. If one of his girls stayed out overnight and showed up late for work the next morning, Garner suspended her for three months. This meant no income for her. God help her if she was caught 'working' during her suspension. The poor man that kept her out late had to answer to George as well… if found!

George Garner's illegal dealings had given him opportunities to deal with East Coast mobsters on occasions. He employed a Cairo local, Bill Harris, as a fall guy on ventures that Garner wasn't sure would end well. Harris, a whiskey runner, idolized George so George had no problem suckering Harris into jobs. While building a reputation with Buster Wortman George kept his 'in' with a few East coast mobsters. George didn't deal with the capos but the soldiers who saw that the capos orders were carried out. He would coordinate trucks hauling stolen dresses and furs from the garment districts of New York to the southern states. Non-descript trucks would haul the stolen garments from New York to New Jersey and be transferred to different trucks that would take the merchandise to Kentucky where Garner would have Harris pick them up and deliver to Cairo. Garner would store half of the dresses and furs in a warehouse he either owned or rented and pay Harris $500 for delivering the stolen goods to him. The other half Harris would transport to Mississippi and receive another $500 on delivery.

Harris almost cut his life short with one delivery by telling a Mississippi dockworker that Garner had paid him

$700. The dockworker, seeing what Harris was up to, showed him the switchblade he carried. Harris willingly accepted just the $500! As Harris was getting in his truck for the return trip to Cairo the dockworker said, "Tell Garner to send someone else, we don't want to see *you* again!"

About 41 miles east of St. Louis is the small, quaint town of Okawville, Illinois. The outstanding attraction of the town was the healing powers of the water that flowed under the town. Drawing people from all over, the water was said to be a cure for arthritis, rheumatism, digestive disorders, and many other illnesses that the best doctors could not cure. The Original Springs Hotel had become famous for the upstairs rooms that held tubs so people could absorb the healing magic of the water.

The years between 1924 and 1932 made the Original Springs Hotel *the* place to be for a week. Okawville became the center for the 'Egyptian Hustlers' convention. Door to door salesmen and backseat entrepreneurs from southern Illinois hit the town with products from St. Louis companies and southern Illinois tradesmen who could turn a piece of wood or iron into something beautiful or useful for the up-to-date housewife.

The convention was manna from heaven for the people in Okawville. Hotels in town were booked well in advance. Restaurants had waiting lists. Stores learned to overstock or the shelves would be bare after the third day.

The nightlife was just as exciting as the day. Dancing to live music brought bands out of St. Louis and sometimes Chicago for the week. Circus performers held acts under big tents for the whole family and airplane rides were available for the attendees. It was nothing for Okawville to draw 30,000 additional people into town during the weeklong convention.

People attending this convention were being entertained and having a wonderful time but the hoods of southern Illinois and East St. Louis were not profiting from the convention. That would have to change.

Outside of Calumet City, Illinois and Hot Springs, Arkansas, East St. Louis was wide open for criminal activity. With the gambling, booze and prostitution lacking legitimate law enforcement control it would be easy to infiltrate another illegal racket. Art and George Garner knew rumrunners were passing around and through Okawville delivering the liquor to East St. Louis so why not have 'hot' racing slips picked up there. Gamblers were everywhere and Okawville was no exception. The bookmaking enterprise was growing as a lucrative racket in other parts of southern Illinois. During the convention, one could only guess how much money the criminal element swindled out of the conventioneers. Art Garner discussed the potential with Wortman who gave his approval and suggested that Shot Winchester be the pickup person. This proved financially productive for Wortman. Shot, a few years out of prison and having a good business head, estimated an automatic raise by delivering racing slips along with the booze. Shot's job was to dispatch bets across the hotbeds of mob territory under Wortman's control. In helping Wortman out, he increased his take with an additional $400 a week during the convention.

Jake Ruben, another area sultan and one of the few Jewish businessmen, owned and operated the El Patio tavern at the junction of Rt. 3 and US 51. A strikingly colorful nightclub, the El Patio drew weekend customers from Chicago, St. Louis, Paducah, and Indianapolis. Ruben, had borrowed money from Chicago mobsters to fund the nightclub but kept their interest small so control of the nightclub would remain his. Another financial supporter of Rubin's was East coast mobster Joe Adonis. Adonis had close business dealings with Charles 'Lucky' Luciano. In spite of Adonis' wealth, he kept a hand in common street crime. Jewelry thefts were a favorite of his. Keeping Adonis involved kept Rubin 'in' with the East Coast mobsters.

The nightclubs in the area carried many of the same names as nightclubs in big cities. Owners or financial supporters of the clubs had connections with mobsters, primarily, in the suburbs of Chicago. Big name mobsters had large financial interests in the clubs. For the big city mobsters it was a cardinal rule *not* to have their names on the deeds. They would front the money but someone else signed the bottom line. Other clubs that Jake Rubin had interest in were The Turf and several years later, The Latin Quarters. Though appearing as a local businessman Rubin had loftier business enterprises. His clubs were just a cover for his more profitable business.

In 1947, Hyman Rubin, Jake's father, cooked up a deal with Lawrence Warehouse Company out of California. Hyman leased a warehouse at 2032 Sycamore Street in Cairo, Illinois for $1 a month. He then turned the building over to Jake. The warehouse was next door to the Rex Liquor Store on Sycamore Street. Hyman and Jake's intentions for the warehouse were to store stolen liquor. The Lawrence Warehouse served as a 'field warehouse'. This meant that in reality it was a financial arrangement. The warehouse company acted as the overseer of the contents in the warehouse that Hyman was leasing. The 'special' contents were not to leave the premises and served as a means for Jake Rubin to secure credit. The contents used as promised security were stored in a certain section of the warehouse. The rest of the contents, closer to the front of the building, were not included in the arrangement and distributed elsewhere. A representative of Lawrence Warehouse Company would occasionally spot-check the contents to verify the agreement. Jake Rubin used this warehouse numerous times for himself and friends over the years, to store stolen garments, cigarettes, guns, and liquor.

Rubin had a lucrative market for tax-free cigarettes. Packages of cigarettes were concealed in trucks under fresh produce. Rubin's truck driver had an invoice for tomatoes or melons in the cab of the truck if questioned by police while returning to Cairo. Some of Rubin's trucks were rented appliance repair trucks that held boxes of cigarettes from Kentucky. Bringing the cigarettes across state lines in this fashion, Rubin avoided being charged with a hijacked item and not paying the state tobacco tax. The cigarettes were stored in warehouses and sold later in Illinois, Missouri, and Indiana. Money generated from selling the cigarettes was transported to the crime bosses in spare tires or in hidden compartments of trucks. Occasionally Rubin spiked his stolen inventory with Cuban cigars hijacked from Tampa, Florida. From the Cairo warehouse, the remaining inventory items were sold to southern and western states at a huge profit. The cigars, however, went to northern Illinois and to eastern states.

Jake Rubin's East Coast crime associates involved him in transporting shipments of stolen weapons. Rubin was notified when shipments of guns, by legitimate gun dealers, arrived in New York. The shipment was designated for delivery to government agencies. A case or two would be removed from trucks, hidden for 6-10 days somewhere between New York and Cairo and the paper work adjusted to look authentic. Most of the guns found their way to Texas with the final destination being Cuba. Jake Rubin was never indicted for running guns.

Illinois served as the 'middleman' for hijacked booze. Hijacked whiskey often came out of the state of Maryland as well as Canada. New legislation had taken away the incentive of a tax-free sale out of the state. When this happened, many of the organized crime figures in Maryland connected with the gangsters in Cairo to fulfill the contracts. Much of the hijacked liquor that Jake Rubin hid in his warehouse originated from Maryland. Both Hymie and Jake Rubin cut deals with J. B. Wenger, a Cairo wholesaler, to ship the liquor into the Southeastern states. Rubin would have his trucks converge on back roads where the shipment would be transferred to flatbed trucks and disguised to look like a regular produce or appliance shipment. Sometimes Rubin used trucks with fake bottoms to conceal the whiskey or creosote-oil trucks with fake tanks. He was careful to cover all bases by having fake invoices prepared for the drivers should they be stopped and questioned. When the delivery reached its destination, a man signed for the delivery making the entire scheme look legitimate. The man that signed the delivery ticket on the receiving end would average $100 dollars a week to accept the delivery with no questions.

Competition in the distribution business was high in Cairo. While the Rubins' were supplying the southern states with stolen liquor, Arthur T. McAboy representing J.R. B. Liquor Company in Cairo was attempting to negotiate a deal with the Raleigh Import Distributors in Chicago. His position with J.R.B. Liquor was assisting in approving monetary loans for liquor import distributors. McAboy wanted a 75% interest in the Raleigh Import Company. He attempted to work the deal so that Thomas Cassara, president of Raleigh Import, would receive 25%. Rocca DeStefano of the Capone syndicate would be a silent partner. Capone would decide DeStefano's cut. To seal the deal McAboy and Cassara ate lunch at a Rush Street restaurant in Chicago discussing the proposal. Upon leaving the restaurant Thomas Cassara was shot for reasons unknown. The deal was put on hold! It is unclear if McAboy pursued the venture to cut a deal with Raleigh Import later but Cairo, Illinois did not suffer from the failed plan; from early 1940 through 1949, 30,000 cases of illegal booze was shipped out of Cairo to dry counties in Georgia alone by the Rubins.

Jake Rubin and the Garner brothers came from religious homes. Their parents and extended family members were faithful to their churches and synagogues. Regular confessions were a family tradition, though as young adults Jake and the Garners saw things differently. Their motto was, "You don't confess to a priest or Rabbi. You light candles and keep your mouth shut!" The mafia was a government and a religion of its own and Jake, Art, and George were faithful followers. Their tribute to the mafia was done by extortion from the common working man and extortion became well practiced in southern Illinois.

Little Egypt may have had a thriving business district but much of it wasn't legitimate. Another icon in both southern Illinois and Western Kentucky was Jewish auto dealer Ben Fishel. The short, stocky man with the sly grin was well liked and respected in the business world. Fishel, who lived at 2841 Park Place West in Cairo, came from St. Louis around the mid 1930's and operated a lucrative Studebaker and Hudson car dealership at 2114 Sycamore Street in Cairo. Dark, stocky, devoted husband and loving father, Ben represented one of the more productive 'black market' businesses in southern Illinois. The business of selling cars to locals and customers from neighboring states provided a comfortable income for his family but Ben sought greener pastures for himself. He had dealerships in Paducah, Bardwell and Mayfield Kentucky as well as Cairo. He maintained a lucrative car salvage business in Murray, Kentucky and Cairo. It was in the salvage yard business that he hid 'extra' cars that would be used in criminal activity. Good friends with Jake Rubin, Ben found just the racket to ensure his personal concept of being wealthy. Jake and Ben provided cars and 'manufactured' car plates to both Missouri and Cairo hoodlums if they needed an unknown vehicle with an out of state license to commit a crime. Law enforcement would be looking for a car that supposedly wasn't from the area.

By the mid 1940's, Joe Adonis had gained financial security in the black market auto deals in New York and Joseph Zirelli had the market in Detroit. This quickly spread across the nation and in 1944, Ben Fishel, a Jewish car dealer, brought it to Cairo, Illinois. Through his connections with Zirelli, Ben offered Detroit car dealerships a deal they couldn't refuse. Ben agreed to take the staggering amount of unsold cars off the lots in Detroit for the ceiling price of $4 million. The purchase wasn't modest at 5,000 cars. Jake Rubin provided the trucks and leased train cars to bring the haul to Fishel's dealership in Cairo, Illinois and Murray, Kentucky salvage lots and auctions. The cars were kept at various locations to not attract the attention of G-men and local law enforcement. Fishel sold his cars for a grand total of $7 million. Law officials expected big cities, big names, and corporations to be ringleaders in the black market not small towns and little dealerships and certainly not in Cairo, Illinois.

The black market thrived during WWII. Everybody turned a deaf ear and blind eye to what was going on. The black market was all about price control of the wanted product. It was another example practiced by war weary people who became as complacent to this as they had to Prohibition.

Ben's plan was to sell the cars to dealers in the southern states where cars were in short supply. Ben was even bringing in the dough while serving his country. He and Ralph Meyer, who inherited the Spur Inn tavern in Karnak, Illinois, were stationed at Fort Knox Army base together and became close friends. According to Ralph, "while most families were financially strapped when husbands were away in the service, Sergeants and Lieutenants in the service were driving new cars they bought from Fishel." Some of the black market cars sold on contract went to Illinois government dignitaries. After nearly 2 years of running the scheme, Fishel was indicted and did time for violating the Price Administration Laws but the car business continued to thrive even with the kingpin behind bars. Was the state government aware that some of Fishel's business was black market contracts? Well, it was *Illinois* and greased political palms were common.

Ben may have been blessed with a sharp financial mind but was forgetful with an indiscretion he had while in the service. Upon arriving back in Cairo after the war his wife, Dorothy, met him with a package that had arrived in the mail a day before Ben arrived home. Within the package was civilian clothing that Ben had left at a woman's home that Ben had been staying with off and on while at Fort Knox. She had graciously sent it back to him with a love letter enclosed. Maybe the war wasn't over!

The public may have bought into Ben Fishel's spotless reputation due to his kindness to local residents and his generous monetary contributions to charities but, his hands were dirty. Buster Wortman, Jake Rubin, and out of state gangsters didn't like the cut they were getting from Fishel *and* the fact that Fishel was a maverick conducting his 'business' *his* way. He was playing both sides…the local gangsters and the mafia. Fishel ignored the warnings he got thinking he had all of them in his pocket. Finally, someone decided Ben Fishel had to go. Wortman's men planned to catch Fishel alone in his home. What they *did not* know was a second team of killers were brought in from the Chicago area the same night.

Entering the back door and coming into the living quarters by way of the basement, the killers waited until Fishel came home from a meeting at this temple. A rope was placed around his neck to bring him down. Once on the floor a blanket was placed over his head to muffle the gun shots. Nothing else was touched or removed from the home. A message was delivered that night.

Later, the same night, a Cairo police officer on patrol noticed an out of town car moving slowly up and down Sycamore Street. The officer pulled the car to the curb and asked the two men in the front seat what they were doing. The driver's response was. "We came to do a job, but someone beat us to it."

Newspapers, at the time, printed what they were told to print about Ben Fishel. It was just enough material to satisfy the reader but was glossed over and much of the truth omitted. The published version kept coins in the paper machines along the street curbs and speculative conversations in the taverns.

All the sultans of Little Egypt became criminals by choice. Most had a legitimate business to begin with but enhanced their income with the illegal addition. To the people living in the area, the sultans of southern Illinois revived the romance of the 'old south'. The gangsters that provided the booze to the public became glorified heroes. The local hoodlums of southern Illinois, who provided 'black market' items, were worshipped. The clever mobsters from big cities knew what they were doing by keeping their names clean through the employment of locals who unwittingly risked their lives to deliver the goods.

MAUREEN HUGHS

The Dens of Vice in Southern Illinois

Nightclubs were moneymakers for organized crime. Mobsters liked the atmosphere and saw the flow of money enticing, especially on weekends. Pulaski and Alexander counties had already earned the nickname of "Little Chicago" in respect to nightclubs. State highway 45 was crowded with cars on Friday afternoon with Chicagoans headed south for the weekend. The St. Louis partiers flooded Route 3 into Mounds, Urbandale, and Cairo. People from Sikeston Missouri and Paducah, Kentucky were regulars at the nightspots in Cairo and along junction 37 and 169 at Karnak, Illinois.

Local people owned all the clubs but most were financially fronted by big city mobsters and deeded to either a relative, close friend or *employee* of a mobster or the local owner(s). By funding the club, the mob had an interest in it or provided protection from law enforcement. This also meant that the mob had a grip on the club owner and could collect 'juice money' or interest from them until the debt was paid. The clubs always had a 'special' room or a block building adjacent to the main structure that housed either gambling equipment, prostitutes or both. The adjacent building was made of concrete block so it would withstand a bombing from a rival, which was prevalent in the area.

Anybody who was anybody and many people who should not have, patronized the clubs on a regular basis. The Tic Toc Club, The Curve Inn, The Thunderbird, Flamingo, Frog City Club, The Colony, 21 Club, El Patio, Casino Club, The Tin Inn, Bell City, Frog City, and The Turf were all well-known casinos. The Turf club, originally owned by the Ryan brothers, was sold to Jake Rubin for $90,000. This sale did not include the liquor stock. The liquor was easily sold, off the books, to 'dry' counties in the southern states. B.B. Harris, George Garner's friend owned The Paradise Club at the north end of Urbandale, Illinois. B.B. Harris had earned an unflattering reputation while owner of The Paradise Club. Everyone knew he would smile to your face and stab you in the back. No one took Harris as a serious friend. On the East side of Route 51, the popular Latin Quarters casino club was a big attraction for the St. Louis crowd. Its reputation was for pricey dining and big name bands before and after Jake Rubin took ownership of it. One of the more notorious casinos was the Purple Crackle, located along route 146 in McClure, Illinois. Its history far outlasted most of the other clubs. The high stakes card, craps, and roulette games were conducted only at the Hotel Cairo in Cairo and later on Club Winchester south of Olmsted, Illinois. The Green Tavern stood outside of Cairo. It was no secret to the locals that Capone had a hit man employed as a bartender there.

With Capone's financial interest in a few of the clubs, it was important to have someone close to rub out someone if *they* were skimming money.

For fifty cents, a ferry brought patrons from Kentucky to Illinois. To keep customers coming back, ferry receipts were reimbursed at the casino door. All the casinos had at least one craps table, one roulette table and a string of slot machines. Big name bands and orchestras brought the crowds in. For the patrons to say that they saw Guy Lombardo or Louis Armstrong justified the dollar door fee. The bands were not cheap for casino owners. Big names drew as much as $10,000 for one evening performance. Generally, the craps tables brought in the most revenue. Club owners decided the bet limits, which usually ranged from $1.00 to $200.00 depending on the game. Missouri cotton farmers were high rollers and club owners treated them like royalty when they came in. Their presence meant large *donations* to the clubs. All the clubs were within a thirty-mile run of each other. They brought wealth to a few in the area and gave the politicians, the sultans of the southern counties and mobsters reason to call the area Million Dollar Row.

Of course, the club owners and mob interests were not the only ones who profited from the casino clubs. Law enforcement officers, lawyers and judges were paid off to look the other way or throw cases out of court if they involved a situation in a particular club. Murray Humphreys, brought big money, from Al Capone, downstate to pay off judges in southern Illinois trials that involved men directly or indirectly employed by Capone. Humphreys, a smooth talker who easily fit in with a 'local' or a politician in Springfield often said, "Money does my business for me."

On January 5, 1937, Cairo and other close communities in Illinois experienced the worst flood ever recorded. Neighboring states were affected too. Seventy percent of Louisville, Kentucky was under water. The force of the water lifted homes off their foundations and moved entire houses out of state. Flooding wasn't a new thing to the area but *this* flood exceeded all others in the past. It had been nearly twenty-five years since the last flood threatened the town. The Ohio River, which was usually high in the winter, spilled over due to an unusual amount of fast melting snow in the mountains of the Northeast. The river raged and nearly covered Cairo in water. No one had prepared for this flood. Fifty-six communities in southern Illinois were involved in the worst flood to date. January temperatures held no mercy as the icy water blended with the freezing temperatures causing sickness and hundreds of deaths.

Shot Winchester left his home in Vienna to help fill sandbags and unload rescue boats from barges. In Missouri, he unloaded train cars filled with supplies and food and drove trucks filled with food and clothing to areas not affected by the floodwaters. People with small boats and canoes would meet him and others to get the supplies into Cairo. It took much longer for medical supplies to reach the thousand homeless residents in Cairo and surrounding areas. Elizabethtown, Rosiclare, and Golconda became an island unto themselves. Neither food nor medical supplies were able to reach the residents for days. A month later, the river water subsided and the cleanup began. By spring, people were back in their homes and businesses had opened their doors once again.

With the horrors of the flood a memory, romance blossomed in the town of Metropolis, Illinois. Shot had met a young woman while driving one of Miller's dairy trucks to Cairo. Mearl Highers and Shot became an item in the area as their relationship advanced. Wedding bells rang on June 29, 1937, when Mearl became Mrs. Lester Winchester in Metropolis, Illinois. She kept her job in Metropolis and Shot continued his bootlegging runs and racing slip deliveries. Together they were bringing in $1,000.00 or more a week. The union between Shot and Mearl did not last long as she died early in the marriage. The cause of her death is not recorded which often happened. Coroners or rural doctors failed to record death certificates in the county court house or the records were misplaced due to a poor system. No known record of her burial place is recorded either.

Shot began investing in real estate after Mearl's death. He already owned two taverns in Vienna and added two houses in Grand Chain, Illinois and about two thousand acres of land between his home town of Vienna and Olmsted. He rented the houses to residents of Grand Chain and the ground to farmers.

The dens of vice were exceptionally profitable in Cairo and surrounding towns. Satch Meyer owned and operated the Spur Inn at Karnak, Illinois, north of Cairo at the intersection of Routes 37 and 169. Dancing was big in his club and a stopover for gangsters out of Chicago on their way to Cairo or their retreats in the southern states. The Spur's menu drew people throughout the week and the weekend.

As many as 400 hundred people attended the Spur's busiest nights when The Glenn Miller band provided the music. Sundays brought the women, dressed in their finest, for 'high tea' and pastries. Linen tablecloths graced with petite flower arrangements welcomed the women as they exchanged the latest gossip and listened to music.

Several years later, in the mid '50's, The Spur Inn hired Chicagoan Jack Ruby as a card dealer. Ruby had tasted crime in California in the early 1930's selling horse racing tip sheets and smuggling marijuana out of Mexico. He returned to Chicago and worked for the local Labor Union in Chicago and the Scrap Iron and Junk Handlers Union local 20467 earning about $23 a week. His union card stated he was a union organizer but in reality, he was a strong-arm enforcer. He had attempted a variety of swindles that had not always included paying the mob their percentage. He had had racket dealings with mob hit man Lenny Patrick. Patrick liked Ruby because he could bring in the money through strong-arm tactics. If Jack Ruby had a fault, it was that he couldn't keep his mouth shut and the Chicago Outfit was tired of it. He took the advice of friends and left for Dallas, Texas to run and later purchase a nightclub he named the Silver Spur. He had illegal money issues that drew the attention of the law in Dallas. Ruby called upon his Chicago friends to help him out. Jack tried to go into business with his brother who was involved in whiskey distribution in Oklahoma. This didn't work out well and Ruby headed back to Chicago. Trying to make a living with the Outfit and keep his wife financially happy, Ruby did work for the mob. He skimmed what he could from Union funds. What he didn't know was that the Outfit was watching him. Lenny Patrick threatened him with "you won't see morning!" Realizing he was in trouble, he headed south and left his wife in Chicago. Ruby's wife traveled downstate to visit Jack but arguments over money or the lack of became a regular purpose for her visits. Jack was constantly looking for ways to increase his cash flow and felt he wasn't going to do it dealing cards at the Spur Inn, in Karnak, Illinois. Hearing that there were jobs out west through his mob connections, he sent his wife home to Chicago and told her to stay there until he could find a better job.

In Texas, he joined an underground group that was running guns to Cuba. He had been nothing but poor and wanted to run with the big dogs and get a piece of the big money. If he had a stake in the Cuban gun running operation, it was small. No one liked Ruby and didn't fully trust him because he could not keep his mouth shut. What friends he did have in Texas used him for their gain. Ruby was known in many states, and eventually Cuba, as a runner for various stolen items other than guns. Always struggling to make the big leagues Jack would offer to be a gofer for the mob or do a hit for them. Shortening his name from Rubenstein to Ruby didn't erase the fact that he was *still* Jewish and not accepted by most mafia members. Whether Jack saw that he was a liability in the gunrunning racket is not clear but for sure, he was not a trusted party in any of the deals. What he was good at was running strip joints and he operated two of them in Texas. The fact that Ruby couldn't keep his mouth shut and his self-esteem issues prevented him from making the big leagues with the mafia. He was a large man with a loud voice but a belittling wife constantly on his back for more money kept him on the edge searching for ways to be a big shot to her and to everyone else. Maintaining a low rung on the ladder for years, Jack Ruby's claim to fame would occur years later in Dallas, Texas.

In the late 1930's, on the northeast corner of Routes 37 and 169, Shot Winchester built the Casino Club on leased land with $7,000 he borrowed from his former employer, Paul Miller of Miller's Dairy. He had a decent business with good food, liquor, and great gambling. He hired Archie Slagle to tend bar and prepare fast food. That spring Shot sponsored a baseball team for the local boys. The baseball field was east and a little north of the Casino Club. The popularity of the games became well known in southern Illinois counties. Shot advertised for neighboring teams to participate in tournaments that drew large crowds of spectators. Newspapers from Cairo to Springfield gave game results and listed the winners. After the games, Shot treated his team to hotdogs and Coke, which on some game days was the best part. One of Shot's regular customers and friend was Paul Powell of Vienna. Paul Powell later made a career in Illinois politics and became a legend.

Late winter 1942, Shot began dating Cora Elizabeth Kimsey of Rosiclare, Illinois. It was a practice among young adults to pile into a car and head for the Curve Inn club in Vienna for an evening of dancing and fun. After the Casino Club was built, the teens would travel to Karnak, Illinois to dance at the club. Needing more employees, Shot hired Cora and her best friend Helen Watson, as waitresses on a part time basis. Sometimes Cora would

56

bring her younger brother with her to tend bar and clean the floor and stockroom at closing time. Archie and Cora's brother were paid $5 each for the weekend work they did. Around 10, PM Sunday night Cora would take Archie and her brother home. However, this arrangement didn't last long. Shot, afraid he would get into trouble due to the boy's age, let the youngster go but kept his friend, Archie Slagle, who had just turned 18, to do the work by himself on a more full-time basis. Archie was paid $25 a week including room and board.

Shot's attentiveness to Cora grew and they began to spend all their free time together through the summer and fall of 1943. On December 31, 1943 in Charleston, Missouri, Shot and Cora married. Cora was 27 and Shot was 49. Because of his prison record Shot could not have a liquor license so Cora's name was on the club's deed. Before that, he had it listed under the name of Mary Sergent who had owned the Flamingo Club in the area.

Archie, who was dating a local woman named Florence for a couple of years, was telling Shot he wanted to marry her. Shot told Archie he would put him through college if he didn't get married.

"Shot kept harping about the importance of an education nowadays. He thought marriage was fine but that I should get an education first then marry Florence. Shot said I was smart and should go on to college and become somebody. I didn't want to hear that. I agreed with Shot but I loved Florence and waiting four years to attend college and then get married was too long. I think I let Shot down. August 29, 1945 Florence and I married at the Casino Club. I was considered family to Shot and Florence was accepted as family too from day one." Archie said.

As the months went by the Casino Club grew in business and became noticed by the unwanted element. Positioned at a major intersection, at the time, people found it a nice stopover when traveling. Archie's responsibilities at the club grew with the increased business and he was often left with handling customers and bar patrons when Shot was doing other chores. Archie told of an incident where he was too trusting of a customer.

"Shot had a small building behind the Casino Club that was used for storing liquor. It had a sturdy door and heavy lock on it. I was young and always saw the good in people...never thinking that there were those out there who made a job out of cheating and lying. One evening a man I had never seen before came into the Casino Club and asked to talk with Shot. I was at the bar washing glasses and remembered that Shot was out in the liquor storage shed taking inventory of the liquor stock that was valued at $9,000. I took the man to the shed and told Shot he wanted to talk with him. When Shot saw who it was he gave me a cold, deathly stare and I immediately knew I had done something very, very wrong. A few minutes later Shot came into the club and called me aside saying to never, never take anyone out to the shed. The man was B.B. Harris, a known contract killer and thief. For the next several nights, until sunup, Shot stayed inside the shed with a shotgun waiting for B.B. to show up, break into the shed, and steal his expensive liquor. Thank God, B.B. Harris never showed up!"

Shot Winchester never wasted time with idle conversation. He was good for a joke and had a keen sense of humor. He did not put up with unruly customers or men who drank too much and tried to start a fight. If a couple of men started an argument, Shot would approach them and quietly ask them to take it outside. Archie remembers a couple of times that being nice didn't pay off.

"Shot only had a couple of incidents that could have been a major problem at the Casino Club. A soldier on leave was in the club. He had been there several hours playing the slot machines and was drunk by the time Shot started moving people out so he could start sweeping the floor. The solider had picked a fight with another customer and Shot separated the two and thought the issue was over. But, the soldier continued to be mouthy and kept pushing the other man. When the soldier wouldn't stop fighting Shot grabbed a broom and broke it over the soldier's head. The soldier came at Shot and Shot took the jagged piece of the broom stick and went for his head again hitting him a couple of times causing the soldier to fall on the floor. Shot helped him up and walked him to the door telling him not to come back. Shot had banged the guy's head up pretty bad. Shot did his own bouncing. He didn't own a gun in the club and never hired anyone else to do it. He would tell known troublemakers to fight outside of the club...not inside the club. He had a reputation of not putting up with troublemakers. What he did have was a couple of pair of flesh colored brass knuckles. Usually, one hit with them straightened his troublemakers out.

Another time a young state trooper came in after his shift. When he came in, he had an ax to grind and let everyone know it. He started a fight with a customer and Shot intervened. Shot took out the flesh colored brass knuckles that he kept in his pocket when he was working in the club. He hit the man twice, and then pushed him into the cigarette machine breaking the glass front on the machine and cutting the man's face in several places. As the bleeding customer left the Casino Club, he vowed to sue but nothing ever came of it. When he sobered up he probably realized he was in the wrong."

Shot was now in a financial position to start making his dream of owning a big nightclub come true. He began to sell off his properties: one of his taverns, his rentals in Grand Chain, Illinois and the two thousand acres of land. With the revenue, he purchased land on the west side of old Route 37 about two miles south of Olmsted, Illinois. The club was to be the biggest nightclub south of Chicago. Shot kept the Casino Club operating and Cora, better known as Izzy to everyone around, was happily pregnant. Working one evening at the Casino Club, Cora went into hard labor. Thinking she would give birth before the ambulance arrived, Cora gracefully climbed onto the craps table between contractions. The ambulance arrived in time. On April 21, 1945, the Winchester's were blessed with a baby boy they named Robert C. Winchester after Shot's father. Shot felt his family was complete and doted on the boy. Seeing that he had a male heir he knew what he would call his nightclub. The nightclub bore the name *Club Winchester* in big neon lights.

In early October, little Bob Winchester, became ill and was diagnosed as having pneumonia. The rural doctor feared that the baby was too weak to survive. Not giving up Shot took his son to a black woman in the swamp lands of Pulaski County. She kept the baby 48 hours treating him with an herbs and oil remedy. At the end of the two days, Shot and Izzy returned to the woman to find their son breathing normally and smiling. Shot never told anyone how the woman specifically treated the baby.

One April 21, 1946, Bob Winchester's first birthday, Club Winchester was dedicated. A huge party was given and attended by local politicians including Illinois legislator and friend Paul Powell. Club Winchester had already earned a reputation for being the finest nightclub around and the personalities and local celebrities that attended the dedication party proved it.

Having enough business at the Club Winchester, Shot sold the Casino Club to Ely and Mary Sergent of Karnak, late 1949. Mary had previously owned the Flamingo Club on Route 3 south of Mounds City and the National Cemetery. Ely was in the well drilling business and had worked part time at the Flamingo Club. In his spare time, he repaired slot machines for several of the clubs in the area. Archie stayed on working at the Casino Club after the Sergents bought it. Mary Sergent paid Archie $35 a week and his wife, Florence, cooked for $20 a week.

Four months after the Sergents purchased the Casino Club, they received word that the landowners wanted to sue the club owners. The building was erected on land owned by two devoutly religious people. The deed to the land stipulated that no alcohol be served or sold on the land. Shot Winchester was unaware of the stipulation and the Sergents, who like Shot had never met the landowners, felt it wouldn't be a problem. To prevent the suit that would stop their business, the club building was raised, placed onto large logs and drug to the southwest corner of the intersection by two teams of horses. To house the prostitutes and the storage of liquor the Sergents constructed a couple of small, one-room buildings behind the club for use. Ely and his wife, Mary lived about 50 yards from the club in a neat, white, non-descript house. Mixed drinks, sandwiches, and dancing provided the entertainment at the club. It was a profitable business but *not* what brought the big money in.

While in the well drilling business, Ely had done work for John Capone, Al's brother. During this period, Ely learned, through John, how to make a lot of money fencing stolen items. By the time he and Mary bought the Casino Club, Ely was a major fence in downstate Illinois. 'Fencing' stolen goods was a well-concealed business in the Cairo area. Sergent was selling stolen jewelry, cigarettes, and pricey liquors to Arthur Vintola in New England. Ely made sure the goods got to Vintola by sending the trucks and cars through the middle or southern part of Ohio and then on to Massachusetts. This route avoided the far-reaching arms of the Chicago outfit that covered northern Illinois, upper Indiana, and Ohio. Ely stored some stolen artwork but because it was hard to unload, kept it to a minimum. The jewelry was brought to Ely by mob friends of Frank Wortman who had stolen the jewelry from wealthy families in Los Angeles. From St. Louis, the jewelry went to Ely to 'hold' for a 'cool down' period. Sergent would keep a piece or two as a 'holder's fee'. From the Casino Club in Karnak, Illinois the jewels made their way to Chicago to Capone's criminal network who insisted that the driver come up to Chicago. Usually, boys that had previously worked for Frank Nitti gave this order. They were completely lost when south of the Chicago suburbs so Ely agreed to make the trip.

Stolen weapons were concealed behind the bar area of the Casino Club and above the ceilings in the little buildings behind the club that housed the prostitutes. .45's were most common though Ely did have a very 'hot' German Mauser and several German Lugers at different times.

Illegal booze was the easiest and quickest item for Ely to fence. Canadian whiskey came out of Detroit to southern Indiana and west to Karnak, Illinois when the heat of law enforcement was too thick along Lake Michigan.

The Sergents kept a hefty supply of counterfeit sugar stamps and cards concealed under a rug in their home. The government issued legal stamps during the war for products not readily available. The Sergent's counterfeit stamp inventory came from Frank Pisciotta of the St. Louis family. When families needed to buy items that were in short supply, like sugar, they would speak to Ely or Mary and soon have the stamp cards in their hands…for a price. Mary kept a small supply of boxed silk stockings stored in their home. The stockings were part of the booty taken in a heist in the New York garment district and kept for special customers or given as gifts to county law enforcement officers if the Sergents heard a raid was going to occur at their club.

MAUREEN HUGHS

Club Winchester

The Club of Distinction

Shot Winchester was finally living his dream. The long years of saving had paid off. All the years of trucking moonshine now history. All the days and nights of trucking Canadian whiskey to East St. Louis or to Danville, Illinois was behind him. Taking betting slips to Okawville was over. He hated cheaters and he hated troublemakers. He didn't have to be on the lookout for hijackers, Prohibition Agents, or hit men. *All* of it was nothing but a distant memory. He was building his dream.

Shot owned an old Ford pickup that he used to bring loads of gravel for the parking lot. Together his friend Archie and he would scoop the gravel and level it on the huge parking area. On nights and weekends the two of them worked on the building long after the contractors left. To the sides and back of the parking lot, Shot designed and planted his beloved flower gardens. The large brick building had a squared off appearance that Shot softened by selecting which trees to save when the parking lot was placed and planting elegant gardens full of rose bushes, dahlias, mums and daises. The profusion of colorful blossoms made for an ambience of enchantment during the day and well into the evening.

The club's bar was custom made from mahogany timbers and became a, much talked about feature by customers. The front of the bar was plush and decorative. The bar stools were made of rich fabric with polished brass legs that sparkled when light hit them. Ceiling titles were acoustical to benefit the big bands that played there.

When the time came for obtaining a liquor license, Shot had Club Winchester put in Archie and Florence's Slagle's name. Shot would never be able to have a liquor license in his name because of his felony conviction. However, he trusted Archie and Florence and was comfortable with the arrangement. The club was a family affair to Shot. He hired many of his relatives to work during the busy weekends. Nieces worked the main door taking in the $1 cover charge on weekends. On other nights, they were hatcheck girls.

Archie purchased liquor from Paducah, Kentucky liquor distributors and delivered it to Club Winchester. Shot stayed away from Cairo liquor distributors for fear the liquor was hijacked. He had a key to the liquor storage room, the club's office, and the front door. That's all. Francis, the bookkeeper, was the only employee who had the combination to the safe. Shot did this as a security measure. Outside, beautiful neon lights were added to the front of the club. The club had taken over a year to build but already the Club Winchester's name was spoken in big cities. This wasn't *just* a tavern or nightclub. This was *Club Winchester!*

The club of distinction.

On April 21, 1946, Club Winchester was formally dedicated. The dedication was a sacred occasion for Shot. For a man that didn't jump to conclusions, was always calm and steady this date, this night, was thrilling for him. The place was packed with close friends, relatives, political friends and people Shot had never met before. It was a night that Shot would never forget.

The club was many times bigger than Shot's previous clubs or any of the other clubs around the southern counties. The Paramount Club in Lakeland, Florida was the only club that could rival Shot Winchester's nightclub. Even the well-publicized clubs of Chicago were not competition. Club Winchester offered a true nightclub atmosphere with top nightclub acts and music.

Shot's close friend from Vienna, Illinois, Archie Slagle, continued to work as a part time bartender at the Casino Club. Shot kept him on when the Club Winchester was formally opened for business to work as a bartender during the week in the beginning. He was paid $51 off the top. No receipt, no bookkeeping. Between what he made at Club Winchester and his part time work at the Casino Club, Archie was making good money for his family. Archie brought James Donithan in to serve as part-time bartender for Shot. Mark Hughes of Olmsted and other high school boys were employed to clean the floors, wash windows, clean the bar on occasions, and police the parking lot for trash.

Behind the Club Winchester, Shot had previously built a row of 10x10, 2-room cabins for the employees. Archie and Florence lived in the furthest north cabin. On the south end of the row, Shot built a 5-room house for himself, Izzy and their son, Bob. This worked well for those who lived several miles away and worked long and irregular hours. Occasionally, Shot would allow a high roller to spend the night in one of the cabins. This was especially true if the high roller had won a jackpot. Shot wanted to protect him if it became widely known that he had won a lot of money. Leaving for home in the morning was a lot safer and Shot would hope he would come back to the club again. Bill Harris, a parolee Shot had befriended and who worked part-time at the club lived there several months while working as a bartender at the club. It also kept the Winchesters together. Before, Izzy had been driving back to Vienna or Rosiclare at night. The long hours at the club and the long drive back grew old for Izzy. She wanted the family home at night and felt their son, Bob, needed that stability on a regular basis instead of living in two different places.

A few months later, though, Izzy grew dissatisfied with this arrangement. She wanted more family time and less hours working at Club Winchester. Shot wanted that too but to keep a business with the grandeur of Club Winchester took hours and hours of work, planning, and preparation. There was rarely a day off for him.

"What time Shot took off from the club he hunted. Shot had two hunting dogs that meant a lot to him." Archie said. "The setter, named Promise was Shot's favorite of the two. Promise was unique in that the dog's tail went at a 45-degree angle instead of straight out when he pointed. It looked funny but the dog was never wrong. If Promise was pointing, you could bet there was a covey of quail in the thicket. I took a picture of Promise in his typical pointed stance with the tail at a 45-degree angle. Shot liked the picture so much he had a sketch of Promise placed on the front of the highball glasses used in the club. On the back of the glasses was the phrase, 'Always forgiven-please come back.' What Shot meant was if you took the glass home don't worry about it…just come back. Sketches of Promise were also on the two large mirrors that hung on the wall behind the bar.

Every year Shot would buy new hunting clothes and give me the old ones. He was just like that. Help anyone he could. He always worked it so he and I could go hunting together."

On one occasion, a semi load of the special glasses was delivered to the Club Winchester about 10 am. The driver went into the club to find someone to pay him as the load was COD. The invoice was for $500. Archie Slagle continues, "The driver said he had to be paid or he would turn around and leave *with* the glassware. Shot was gone for the day. I was the only person there and I didn't have any money on me and I couldn't get into the register. I told the truck driver to sit at the bar and have a beer while I tried to get the money. I jumped in my truck and drove the 2 miles to Olmsted. The only person I knew that had that kind of money was E.C. Hogendobler, President of the Olmsted bank in Olmsted, Illinois. I walked in and told him what I needed and why. Without batting an eye, E.C. went to the cashier and took $500 out of her drawer and handed it to me. I didn't have to sign anything! When Shot returned to the club I told him what I had done and he said, "You did what!" He grinned and shook his head. He opened the bar register, took $500 out and drove into Olmsted to repay the bank."

White linen tablecloths were purchased for each of the tables. White starched short coats for the bartenders and pretty costumes for the hatcheck girls. The opulent splendor of Club Winchester vividly portrayed the glitz and glamour of the era.

Shot Winchester had spent years dreaming of his club. Archie said of Shot, "He was naturally a personable individual and very sensitive to people who worked for him. He made everything happen at the club. He spent hours upon hours at the club, working out details of upcoming entertainment, inventory of food and liquor, cleaning the club and making sure uniforms were clean and starched and fresh flowers from his beautiful flower gardens on every table every weekend night."

The man behind the Club Winchester was realizing his lifelong field of dreams. He could converse with anyone from any social level and was an attentive listener. Whether they were affluent or dock workers for local barge companies on the Ohio or Mississippi Rivers, Shot could talk with them. He mingled with the wealthy and political scions and made everyone feel comfortable and welcomed. If the wealthy were stuffy and the politicians somewhat unapproachable, Shot would introduce them to people in other social levels making them acquainted with each other. He never flattered himself and remained humble and mercurial about his club. Club Winchester was Shot's sanctuary. This was partly due to necessity but mostly because it was his. People would remember him because of Club Winchester. It was *his* lifetime dream. He was happy just to be in the club and to him the work it involved *was* happiness.

Shot remembered that as a youth he had fallen from grace because he was cheated at a game of dice. He hated cheaters! If the young man had returned the money he cheated Shot out of all would have been forgotten. That would have been the end of it. However, the lad lied and lied to Shot. He hated liars too. Calling his mother vulgar names crossed the line for him. He could take no more. Shot's abhorrence for cheaters, liars, and troublemakers started when he was very young and stayed with him throughout his life.

The issue of not having a normal family life became a breaking point for Izzy. She and their son, Bob moved back to Rosiclare to be closer to her family. In Rosiclare she rented an apartment within a Federal housing project called Spar Dale that had been constructed for families of Spar Dale miners during WWII. She obtained employment at the local 5 and 10 department store. Shot drove back to Vienna only once a week to have dinner with his friends Archie and Florence. He made efforts to see Izzy and Bob and attempted to convince her to move back but Izzy could not cope with the demands of motherhood and the strain of operating the nightclub. The relationship between Shot and Izzy became noticeably strained. In an attempt to keep the family together, Shot built a small house across the highway from Club Winchester. Izzy would not have it. She wanted to stay closer to her family and people she knew. Shot rented the little house to a man by the last name of Ford and his two daughters. The father worked for Shot and others in the area doing odd jobs. One of the daughters, LaVera Mae Ford helped in the kitchen off and on when needed on busy weekend nights.

Big name bands made regular appearances to a packed house at the club. When the music started the dance floor was full. Red Ingle, the comic musician, drew crowds from miles around. He was born with the gift of comedy. No one had to write material for him it just came naturally. By his late teens, Ingle was listed with touring jazz legend Frankie Trumbaurer. Soon he joined up with Ted Weems in 1931 and remained with him until WWII broke out. Singer Perry Como, who sang with the Weems orchestra, said, "Ingle was one of the most talented men I had ever met." Ingle later joined Spike Jones, which set the stage for Ingles' fame. When Jones was performing in Cape Girardeau or St. Louis, Red Ingle would drive over for a guest appearance at the Club Winchester, which thrilled the crowd.

Ted Weems and his orchestra made two known appearances at Club Winchester. Jimmy DeAugustine, drummer for the band for years said, "Ted was a great boss, but had one hang up. He liked to gamble. On one tour at Club Winchester, Shot Winchester paid Ted the nightly fee at the half-time break. This was a common arrangement with all club owners and the bandleaders. Ted took the money and started gambling, losing all of it. When Shot heard this, he personally went to musicians in the orchestra and paid them out of his own pocket. That was the upstanding man Shot was. We all enjoyed him and his club. He was good to us personally and treated Ted very well."

Ernest Tubb and his Country Band were always popular with the Club Winchester fans. Many fans who were regulars at the club related to the singer's simple upbringing. Ernest's parents were sharecroppers in Texas and Ernest knew what hard work was and the value of the dollar. Ernest also brought a new style of music called Honky Tonk to the club. The younger people loved it.

Johnny Lang, the left-handed violinist drew crowds at every appearance. His performance lasted from 9pm-1am. Other nights Canadian dance bandleader Billy Bishop entertained a packed house. The big name entertainers kept the Club Winchester full and at a handsome price of $1,800-$3,000 a night.

One of the most popular orchestras in the nation was Jan Garber and his 12-piece band that offered the best 'swing' music anywhere. King of the one-night-stand contract concept among dance orchestras, Jan signed a *two*-night contract with Club Winchester due to the number of people who were turned away the first night he performed. After his contract was completed with Club Winchester Jan signed a permanent contract with the Desert Inn in Las Vegas until his retirement.

Archie Slagle remembers Jan Garber's arrival at Club Winchester. "Jan Garber's truck pulled up to the northeast corner door of the club. This door opened to the performance stage. A man in a torn t-shirt and dirty slacks came out of the garden and helped the band unload the truck and set up their equipment. When everything was inside and set up on the stage, Jan went to the bar requesting Archie take him to meet Shot Winchester. I told him he already had. He was the man in the torn shirt and dirty slacks that helped you unload and set up. Jan Garber said, "Oh my God...I tipped him $1!" Jan and Shot had a good laugh over it but Shot kept the dollar bill just the same."

Nightclubs offering an elegant dinner and ballroom dancing were a welcome escape for war weary Americans. People filled dance floors across the nation dancing the Fox Trot, Samba, Tango, Rumba and local styles of the Swing. The federal government, seeing the popularity of the nightclub business, levied a 'Cabaret Tax' of 30% on any club that had big bands and ballroom dancing in 1944. The country needed money after the war and taxing the multimillion-dollar nightclub business was one way to make some. For months, arguments broke out in legislatures across the nation over what constituted ballrooms and entertainment with music. Most club owners went along with the tax when learning that it would be lifted in 1947. Instead of lifting the tax at the expiration time, the government extended it forcing some clubs to close or increase the cost of food to compensate for the cabaret tax that was *forced* upon them.

People came from states on both sides of the Mississippi River and spent the weekend within Pulaski or Alexander counties when big bands like Ted Weems or the Tommy Reynolds Orchestra were at the Club Winchester. One hotel in particular was both popular *and* colorful reputationwise. The Rosalyn Hotel in Cairo, formerly the Kennedy Hotel, was owned and operated by Roselyn Waite. She purchased the beautiful hotel at 611 Washington Street around 1946 or 1947. It was an upscale hotel and served as the place to stay for Art Garner when he had 'business' in Cairo. Art and Mrs. Garner had a special room that was reserved especially for them. Rosalyn, the beloved owner, hid many gangsters in the basement of the hotel when the

74

law was on their tail. Rooms went for $2 or $3 dollars a night. If a known mobster was renting the room, it was *always* $3. One of the special guests, prior to Waite's ownership, was Al Capone. He spent several nights at the hotel when doing business in southern Illinois or on his way to Florida. To compensate for his misdeeds Capone would place a hundred dollar bill in the 'poor plate' within St. Patrick's Catholic Church across the street from the hotel. Even a few Cairoites reserved rooms for their line of work or for refuge from the local law enforcement. Regulars at the hotel referred to the owner as 'Momma Waite' because she was so kind and giving to everyone who stayed there. Many secrets and ghosts were left behind the hotel's walls over the decades.

Shot, on occasion, would stop at the Rosalyn Hotel while in Cairo to pick up supplies or on his way to Paducah to pick up additional linen tablecloths for the club. Sometimes he took Bill Harris, who helped at the club doing odd jobs and minor repairs when not bartending. Bill usually ordered a beer but Shot only drank Cokes. He never drank anything stronger.

Archie talked about Shot's drinking. "A Jewish salesman stopped at Club Winchester selling Mogan David wine. He and Shot went to the bar and the salesman poured Shot a glassful of the wine. Shot brought the glass to his lips but didn't take any in his mouth. He left the glass on the bar. Shot had Jewish customers from Cairo so he agreed to purchase the wine. The two of them went to the salesman's truck and the driver handed Shot a case. Shot paid him in cash."

Most of Shot's customers were people he knew or

would come to know from repeated visits to the club. One man in particular would be seen on occasion sitting by himself and often wearing sunglasses. He was Joseph Aiuppa from Chicago. Aiuppa owned a Chicago furniture business, which, in reality, was a front for a slot machine manufacturing business. He was a partner in a gambling equipment company outside of Chicago and served as one of the directors of Cicero's Bartender's Union. He would talk briefly with Shot and then leave. He was never seen gambling but would watch over the craps table for a short period.

Anthony Accardo, known to the mafia as "Joe Batters", frequented Club Winchester with his wife, Clarice. This was the stop over for Accardo when he had a meeting with Murray Humphreys in St. Louis. After a night of dining and dancing the Accardo's would head for St. Louis in the wee hours of morning. While at Club Winchester Tony would exchange pleasantries with Shot Winchester but there was never any business dealings between the two.

A former member of Capone's Outfit, Accardo would, eventually, replace Sam Giancana as head of the Chicago crime family.

Another man who frequented the club was Art Garner. He and Mrs. Garner would arrive for a late dinner and some dancing. He would speak briefly to Shot or give a wave to him as they left the club. A few years later Shot would meet with Art, at Art's request, to discuss a business proposition. It was never learned what the subject was. However, the meeting was brief.

On Sundays, business was slower and Shot had someone to cover for him while he drove to Vienna to have sup-

76

per with Archie and Florence. Afterwards he would drive to Rosiclare and spend the night with Izzy and Bob. Sometimes Shot would take Bob back to the club with him the following morning, keeping him there for the day. Bob loved staying at the club. He had a tricycle and rode it around and around the dance floor. Shot had bought Bob a Roy Rogers hat and gun that delighted the young lad and Club Winchester became the Wild West on many occasions.

Employees set a table and chair in front of the stage for Bob to sit at while the weekend entertainment would rehearse. The bartender, on duty would mix a concoction of Pepsi, Coke, and 7-UP in a cup with a little colorful umbrella and give it to Bob. Bob and his little Dashund, Herman, would sit quietly and watch the performers go through their routine on stage.

Other times Bob was a typical kid raising havoc within the club. Shortly after Club Winchester opened, a patron had paid his outstanding bar tab with a genuine, beautifully carved Siamese saber. The saber with a pearl handle was worth more than the bar tab but Shot took into consideration interest on waiting for the tab to be paid and accepted it as even trade. When Bob could get to the saber, he would drag it behind him while riding his tricycle on the dance floor. This was fine except when he accidently stuck a customer, sitting at the bar, in the butt. The customer, Jim Henshaw, took the incident well and nicknamed Bob Winchester 'Butch'. The nickname stayed with Bob. The saber, however, was put in a safe place *out* of Butch's reach!

Archie said of Butch, "Occasionally, Sunday nights was reserved for strippers at Club Winchester. The girls would rehearse Sunday afternoon with Butch sitting in the front row at his table. The girls would tease Butch and throw their outer clothing at his table. Butch had no idea what was going on but felt very important that the strippers would single him out. Of course, there was a good reason for that. Butch was the only one around watching the rehearsal."

Like all the clubs in southern Illinois, Club Winchester had slot machines and gambling tables. The basement held the liquor storage area and all the gambling equipment. Slot machines lined the outer walls. The beautiful roulette and craps tables sat on the basement floor and had customers all night long. Shot didn't know anything about gambling. He really didn't want to. A couple of trusted, knowledgeable craps dealers he knew took care of the craps tables and the roulette table. The slot machines and tables were already rigged by a 'mechanic' when bought by Shot. He preferred providing delicious food and top name entertainment. He had someone else take care of the slot machines and he took a percentage of the take from them. If there were problems with the slot machines, Shot would have Ely Sergent repair them. Shot made sure he knew who was fixing the machine and never used any of Buster Wortman's men. This act made Wortman's men furious but Shot would ignore them and say he didn't have problems with *his* machines.

Mary Sergent's brother-in-law was a part time craps dealer from St. Louis. Shot employed him to work the Club Winchester's crap table on busy weekends because he didn't know anything about the game but wanted knowledgeable dealers to run it. After closing time, Archie Slagel would ask the dealer how they did but the dealer would never admit the dollar amount the craps game brought in. Archie always wondered if the dealer was skimming from what was taken in.

Illinois Governor Greene, to appease the public, would fine Club Winchester and other clubs in the area every three to four weeks. This rarely amounted to much but kept the public satisfied that gambling was being controlled. Indeed it was. The politicians took a percentage of the fine money for their own use not to mention what they got when they showed up at the clubs with their hand out.

Violence was rarely seen at the club. Mark Hughes told relatives that on a weekend night when he was washing bar glasses, a man drew a gun at the craps table. Shot walked over to the man and whispered a few words in his ear. The man put his gun away and left.

Early one morning Shot was in the basement preparing to take the daily liquor inventory when he noticed the basement door to the gambling room was unlocked and slightly ajar. Looking inside Shot saw that someone had attempted to steal the slot machine money. Shot called his friend, State Trooper Don Evers, to witness the sight. On the floor by the slot machines was a 10-gallon container full of coins from the machines. It was obvious that when the thief tried to lift the full container he couldn't due to the weight and left it there on the floor. Both Shot and Evers had a good laugh over the scene. Shot did not file a report but believed the would-be thief was a part-time bartender from Cairo who had a key to the basement and his friend, a part time hair stylist.

"Club Winchester had been robbed only a couple of

times." Said Archie Slagle. "The worse was on a Thursday night late in the fall of 1950; a man came into the club and ordered a Budweiser. He sat there, silently drank the beer then left. Less than an hour later Shot was standing behind the bar cutting flowers and placing them in vases for his tables when the phone rang. Shot answered the call. "How much did they get? Describe the vehicle again." Shot asked. "When Shot hung up I asked what happened. Shot told him and the other employees sitting around the bar that the White Castle Nightclub in Herrin, Illinois had been robbed the previous night. No sooner had Shot finished telling us about the robbery when a truck came speeding up to the front door throwing gravel that went high enough to hit the club windows. Seconds later in rushed two Negro men wearing handkerchiefs on their faces, gloves on their hands and waving pistols. Shot, still behind the bar, gently removed his large diamond Elks ring from his finger and slowly walked over to a stack of empty beer cases under a fuse box mounted on the wall. I and the other employees stood frozen with fear."

One of the robbers said to Archie, "Are you the bartender?"

"Yes, answered Archie."

"Where is your boss, Little Joe Caplan?" Archie replied saying, "There isn't a Joe Caplan here. *That's* my boss." Archie pointed to Shot who was still behind the bar.

"We aren't going to hurt you son. Just stand there." One of the masked robbers said to Archie.

Walking over to the bar the robber said to Shot, "I want you to turn off all the lights…just like you would do when you are closing up. Don't do anything different." As Shot turned to cut the lights from the fuse box, he dropped the ring in his hand behind the empty beer cases. As the robber turned to instruct the employees to sit on the floor Shot dropped a roll of money that was in his pocket behind the empty beer cases. The robber never saw him do it. After the lights were out Shot was instructed to lead one of the robbers to the basement where the safe was. Inside the office, the two went to the corner where the safe sat.

"Open it!" Instructed the thief.

"I can't. I don't know the combination," Shot said.

"What?"

"I have never known the combination."

"Who does then?"

"My bookkeeper," answered Shot.

This infuriated the thief. He took his .45 and struck Shot hard on the head.

"Get the bookkeeper!" The robber yelled.

Shot led the way back upstairs with the gun pressed in his back and instructed Francis Stoltz, his bookkeeper, to go to the basement and open the safe. Once the safe was open, the robber reached in and took the $1,600 that was inside. When everyone was upstairs one of the thieves said that they intended to hit the club the night before but heard dogs barking ferociously close by and decided not to. What they heard was Shot's hunting dogs; they were penned up by the club's back door. All the employees were instructed to stay on the floor for five minutes after the two had left. After the employees could no longer hear the truck one of them rushed Shot to Doc. Robinson in Mounds, Illinois to stitch the wound. Shot learned later that the robbers fit the description of the two black men that robbed the White Castle in Herrin."

Besides the gambling and big name bands that appeared at Club Winchester, the cuisine brought people with an appetite for some of the best food around. The club specialized in Chinese and American food. T-Bone steaks, flanked sirloin steak, Pork chops, Veal cutlets, and fried chicken were the favorites. Shot's cook, Big Eva, known for her southern pan-fried chicken, was a robust, black woman who never had a bad word to say about anyone. She had a habit of coming to work early so she could sit at the bar, eat Hershey candy bars, and drink beer until time to go to work. Shot had her picture put on the front of the club's menu. George Huey prepared the Chinese dishes. His specialty was Sub Gum Chop Suey. Both worked at the club until it closed. Francis Stoltz started her employment as the bookkeeper as the club was being built.

LaVera Mae Ford had become the sweetheart at the club. The employees and regular customers nicknamed her Sissy. She was a vibrant, personable, young woman, working most weekends as extra help in the kitchen. As a senior in high school, Sissy wanted to attend her prom. Not having a prom dress to wear for the occasion the employees at the club chipped in enough money for her to buy a dress and dress shoes. Her classmates remember Sissy as being a beautiful and charming girl.

About 1952 LaVera Mae started dating Shot. He and Izzy had been separated for several months. They saw each other regularly and remained on good terms. She was still living in Rosiclare and continued working at a 5 and 10-cent store in Vienna. She was dating Bill Wendall from the area but the relationship wasn't serious. One night a

82

drunk driving north on the new route 37 lost control of his car and crashed into the house the Fords had been living in. The house caught fire and burned to the ground. LaVera's father and younger sister moved to Metropolis and LeVera Mae moved in with Shot who was living in one of the cabins behind the club.

Lester Winchester home in Vienna, IL
L to R: Lester, Bernard, Earnest

Lester 'Shot' Winchester, age 15, inmate at Menard Penitentiary.

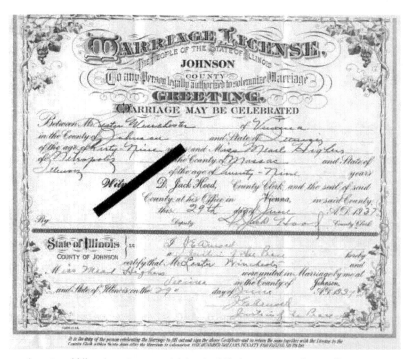

Lester Winchester and Merle Highers marriage license.

Gangster George Garner after his arrest for the murder of Jake Rubin.

MAUREEN HUGHS

Frank 'Buster' Wortman. St. Louis gangster

Carl Shelton of the notorious Shelton gang in southern Illinois.

Coroners death certificate for Clate Adams of Olmsted, IL

Official death certificate for Clate Admas.

Tavern Operator Brutally Slain by Two Men Who Shoot at Wife and Kill Big Dog

2/24/5

Clate Adams, 57, operator of the Tin Inn tavern two miles south of Olmsted on Route 37, was shot to death about 11 p.m. Thursday in the tavern in what was termed a brutal, unprovoked slaying. Adams' faithful 200 pound Great Dane was slain with his master and Mrs. Adams missed death by inches as one of the two men involved fired at her as she attempted to phone for help.

Officials were at a loss to explain the motive for the slayings, although Mrs. Adams indicated that the men probably intended to rob Adams. She said, however, there was nothing said to indicate a robbery when she retired for the night only a few minutes before the shooting started.

The two men fled south by auto and no official report of their apprehension has been made.

Mrs. Adams, nearly incoherent from shock, told the following story.

She said the two men, both young and dressed in work clothes, came into the tavern about 10:30 p. m., shortly before closing time. They sat on stool at the bar and ordered a beer.

They were arguing between themselves when Mrs. Adams turned the television off. One of the men was quoted as saying, "What did you do that for." Mrs. Adams replied that there would be no more programs on the local station and that it would soon go off the air for the night. The man answered sullenly, "Well, I don't like to be pushed around."

Mrs. Adams said she thought nothing of the remark. She then told her husband that she was going to bed. She left for the family living quarters adjoining the north end of the tavern which opens into an area way behind the bar.

Mrs. Adams said that she had just gotten her pajamas on when the firing started.

As she rushed into the bar she heard her husband shout to her in effect, "They're going to kill me, get my gun."

The sequence of events from this point on were hazy. Mrs. Adams said the men were still firing when she entered the tavern. Adams, shot twice in the chest, was crawling toward the tavern living quarters to obtain the gun. The Great Dane, known as a faithful watch dog, rushed into a hallway at the rear of the bar from his sleeping quarters and met death before he reached his master. A single bullet caught the dog in the jugular vein.

Mrs. Adams grabbed for the phone as her husband, mortally wounded, obtained his gun. When Mrs. Adams started phoning, a bullet narrowly missed her. In fleeing, the gunman sent another bullet into Adams' back. Adams managed to get a off a shot through the door at the fleeing

Newspaper articles on Clate Adams murder, Feb. 1956.

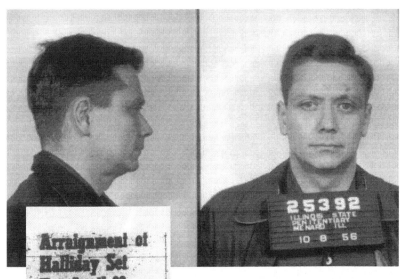

Norman Halliday after arrest for
Clate Adams murder

Arraignment of Halliday Set For April 23

The arraignment of Norman R. Halliday Jr., 33, Cairo, on the charge of murder in the robbery-slaying of Tin Inn tavern operator, Clate Adams on February 23, has been set for Monday, April 23 at 10 a.m. before Circuit Judge Harold L. Zimmerman, who will preside at the April term of Pulaski County Circuit Court.

Halliday's accomplice in the slaying, Alfred Leroy Reahm, alias Al Masters, pleaded guilty to the murder, waived trial by jury and was sentenced to serve 180 years April 5 by Circuit Judge C. Ross Reynolds, Vienna, who also stipulated in the sentence that Reahm be placed in solitary confinement every Feb. 23 to reflect on his crime.

Reahm, in testimony before a grand jury, implicated Lester (Shot) Winchester, 59, Olmsted, operator of Club 37 located about one-half mile south of the Tin Inn, in the Adams slaying. Winchester was found fatally wounded the day after the jury returned a murder indictment against him.

Halliday's case is also set for jury trial on Tuesday, April 24. He is represented by Atty. Joe Crain, Mound City, and Atty. John Holland, Cairo. State's Attorney Loren H. Boyd will be assisted by Atty. Fletcher Lewis, Murphysboro.

A Coroner's inquest into Winchester's death is still pending the results of tests by the State Crime Department.

Other cases set for the April term are:

Non-jury, Dorothy A. Wolter vs. William J. Wolter. Pleading, Adam Heinie, adm., vs. Clarence H. Pirtle Jr.

Newspaper article on N. Halliday's arraignment

SUSPECTED SLAYER CHARGED WITH MURDER — Alfred Leroy Reahm, alias Al Masters, 37, Cairo, center, was formally charged with murder Saturday in the fatal shooting of Clate Adams, 57, operator of the Tin Inn tavern, in a robbery attempt February 25. Reahm is flanked by Frank Clifford, special investigator to Cairo Mayor Paul Baur, left, and Pulaski County Sheriff Robert Aldrich. It was Clifford who identified the gun as one belonging to Reahm, breaking the case three hours after it happened. Reahm's accomplice in the planned hold-up, Norman Halliday Jr., 33, Cairo, charged Reahm with the slaying in a signed confession.

Alfred Reahm (middle) after his arrest for murder of Clate Adams. Feb. 1956

Newspaper article on the murder of Ben Fishel in 1960.

"TEMPORARY"
COUNTY RECORD

STATE OF ILLINOIS
CORONER'S CERTIFICATE OF DEATH

Alexander COUNTY, ILLINOIS

Cairo 25 Yrs.

2841 Park Pl. West 20 years

Ben Fishel Nov. 9, 1960

male white married Feb. 15, 1913 47

owner of Auto Agency Automobile St. Louis, Mo. USA

Isadore Fishel Mary Smith

yes World War II unknown Manfred F. Rosenberg son in law

3121 Park Place West
Cairo, Illinois

MEDICAL CAUSE OF DEATH

Inquest Pending

Gun Shot Wounds

11-9-60

at his home Cairo Alexander Ill.

Roy Keith
11-10-60 Howard B. Stuckey 11/11/60 11-10-60 by: Dep. Connell Smith
Berbling-Marcher
325-6th St., Cairo, Illinois
St. Louis, Missouri B'Nai-Amona
Joe F. Berbling 11-6178

Coroner's death certificate for Ben Fishel.

Ben Fishel's ad on back of Talent Show program in Cairo. 1951

Ben Fishel's car lot in Cario, Il.

This Certifies that

LESTER WINCHESTER   of

KARNAK   State of   ILLINOIS

and   CORA ELIZABETH KIMSEY   of

KARNAK   State of   ILLINOIS

Were United in

Holy Matrimony

Marriage certificate of Lester Winchester and Cora Kimsey.

Winchester Inquest Set For Tonight

A Coroner's Inquest into the death of Lester (Shot) Winchester, 59, Olmsted, operator of the Club 37 tavern, who was found mortally wounded April 7 in his car on an abandoned section of old Route 37 three miles south of Olmsted, under mysterious circumstances, will be held tonight at 7:30 p.m. in Alexander County court house in Cairo under the direction of Coroner Paul Baur.

The inquest has been delayed pending the results of tests by the State Crime Department.

Winchester died in St. Mary's Hospital about 13 hours after he was found with a bullet wound in the head which entered over the right ear. A .38 caliber revolver which had been fired three times was found on the floor of the car. There was a bullet hole near the center of the right front door glass and another in the right corner of the rear window. The left front door glass was rolled down. The wounded man was slumped face down on the front seat with his head under the steering wheel.

At the time Winchester was found he was being sought by Pulaski County Sheriff Robert Aldrich for arrest on a bench warrant ordered issued by Circuit Judge C. Ross Reynolds, Vienna, following Winchester's indictment for murder in aiding and abetting in the death of Clate Adams, 57, Olmsted, who was slain in a robbery attempt Feb. 23.

Winchester had been free on $9,000 bond under an indictment returned in July, 1955 charging him with nine counts of receiving stolen property.

He was implicated in the Adams slaying by Alfred Leroy Realm, 32, alias Al Masters, Cairo, who pleaded guilty to the charge of murder and was sentenced to serve 180 years.

Lester Winchester's Inquest article.

Ted Weems entertainment ad for Club Winchester in Olmsted, IL. Singer Perry Como sang with this orchestra.

Tommy Reynolds and his orchrastra had several engagements at Club Winchester.

Ray Pearl performed at Club Winchester.

Spur Inn in Karnak, Il entertainment ad.

Sherman Hayes performed at Club Winchester

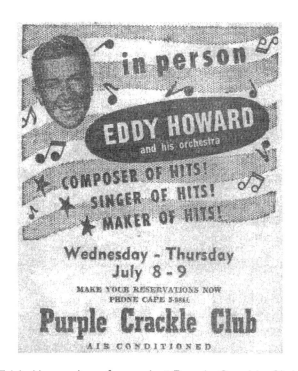

Eddy Howard performed at Purple Crackle Club.

Entertainment contract from Club Winchester.

St. Mary's Infirmary in Cairo, IL.

MAUREEN HUGHS

Stationery from Club Winchester in Olmsted, IL.

Stationery from Casino Club in Karnak, IL.

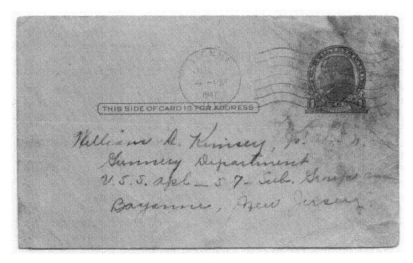

Post card to William Kimsey.

Ely and Mary Sergent sitting in their Casino Club. They pur-
hased the club from Lester Winchester.

Thunderbird nightclub.

Moonshine raid in Metropolis, IL.

"Numbers" board confiscated during raid at local club.

Gambling equipment removed from Club Winchester in Olmsted, IL. Capt. Elza Brantely on left.

St. Police burning gambling equipment confiscated in So. Il.

Police removing gambling equipment including a pistol
from Club Prevue.

Lester Winchester's Coroner's certificate

Newspaper article on inquest verdict.

MAUREEN HUGHS

Archie and Florence Slagle.

Lester 'Shot' Winchester in front of Club Winchester.

Front of Club Winchester from parking lot.

Club Winchester's six bartenders in formal attire. Dee
Donithan 3rd from left.

Dee Donithan cutting up in front of Club Winchester.

Lester Winchester behind the bar at his Casino Club in
Karnak, IL.

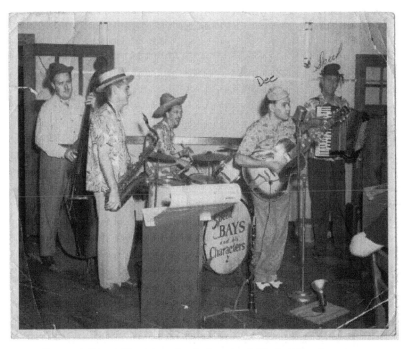

Speed Bays Band entertained at Club Winchester.

Club Winchester's menu.
Eva, the cook on menu face.

Club Winchester's menu. Notice the prices in the 1950's.

MAUREEN HUGHS

Shot Winchester's '56 two-tone Olds. Note bullet hole in passenger window.

'56 Olds. Believed to have been moved, by someone from actual place of crime.

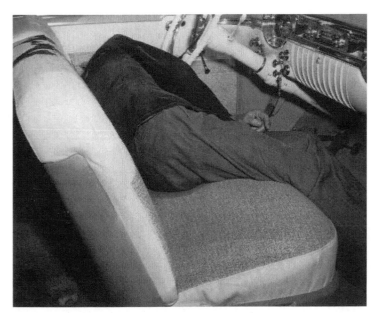

Shot Winchester after being shot. Legs have been moved by someone, from original place. Originally they were on the seat.

Crime photo of driver's side. Engine was still running when first found and radio playing.

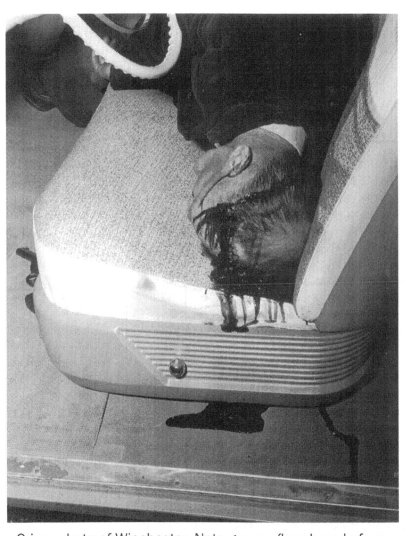

Crime photo of Winchester. Note gun on floor board of car.

Crime scene photo. Notice back glass shot out. Driver's window has been rolled up some by someone.

Bob Winchester's State of Illinois business card. Son of Lester 'Shot' Winchester.

Back entrance to Ben Fishel's house in Cairo, IL. Killers entered here.

Front entrance of Ben Fishel's house in Cairo, IL.

Shot Winchester outside his home in Vienna, IL

MAUREEN HUGHS

Shot sitting on hood of truck.

Lester Winchester's head stone in Vienna, IL where he is buried.

MAUREEN HUGHS

The Hijacking Business

Anyone in the trucking business carried high insurance premiums to cover themselves against hijacking. High demand items like cigarettes, booze and women's clothing and furs topped the list. In 1920, New York added the first tax to cigarettes. When the idea to tax such items spread westward insurance companies raised premiums for trucking companies because of the increase in hijacking. Trucking companies either took the loss out of year-end profits or carried additional insurance. Peter D. of Kansas City, Missouri told why the hijacking of liquor and cigarettes was so lucrative.

"Alexander and Pulaski counties were well located in the state for importing and exporting a variety of commodities and goods. Hijacking became a natural sub-occupation for the region because of that. Cairo, Illinois served as a prime area to pass hijacked liquor through to avoid taxes. The distilleries pay the Federal tax before the liquor gets to the 'export-houses' in places like Cairo. The export houses conducted no domestic business but dealt in the export business to dry states. Sending it out of Illinois also allowed them to pay state taxes on the product. My father and uncles knew Tony Giardano of St. Louis. Tony was small potatoes in the beginning but was connected to people who knew mobsters in New Orleans. Tony was good for keeping his mouth shut and had a boyish, innocent face. Through his connections, he got a fat supply of counterfeit tax stamps that he sold to Wortman and the Garner brothers to place on truckloads of cigarettes. They would pull a truck of stolen smokes in a friends garage and spend all night putting stamps on them! Same with booze only they were more careful with the liquor 'cause the cops were *always* on the lookout for that. Once the stamps were on a driver would haul the stuff to Cairo, Illinois to store in Mr. Rubin's warehouse. I think his father owned the warehouse or part of it. I remember my uncles saying that Mr. Rubin's son, Jake, was a son-of-a bitch. He would sooner shoot you than look at you. I don't know if my uncles had ever worked for Mr. Rubin or not. Just said they didn't like Jake Rubin. Most of the distilleries used rented or leased trucks to transport whiskey and other liquors to the sales outlets. If I remember right Tony got caught and did time for the stamps."

The George Mueller Wholesale Liquor business, in Springfield, Illinois was one exception. Mueller had had his own trucks and a couple of regular drivers. Marty Swanson, a stepson to a former hijacker told this story.

"Herschel Helm worked for Mueller as a driver from the home office. Mueller had Helm to drive to Lawrenceburg, Indiana to pick up a shipment of liquor at the Schenley Distilling Company. Pretty sure it was over 500 cases of whiskey valued at $22, 000. On the return trip, Helm was to stop in Cairo at the J. B. Wenger Company and drop off some of the whiskey." It is assumed that Mueller instructed Helm to make this stop though no proof could be obtained. Swanson continued, "Late at night, on December 29, 1949, Helm left Springfield and arrived at Lawrenceburg early the next morning. Workers at Schenley Distilling loaded the 500 cases onto the Mack truck with Helm watching. He left the distillery at noon on Dec. 30, driving west to Illinois. Instead of heading to Paducah, Kentucky and then up to Cairo, Helm drove north to Vienna, Illinois, forty miles north of Cairo, with his cargo. Helm stayed at a small trucker stop and hotel leaving his truck alongside highway 146."

It is believed that the decision to go to Vienna for the night was Helm's as there were several hotels and motels in Cairo to stay at and he would have been only minutes away from the J. B. Wenger Company.

Marty Swanson continued, "Leaving Vienna on Dec. 31, about 7am, Hershel Helm proceeded south on Route 37 heading for Cairo. About 15 minutes into his trip, a car pulled along the left side of the truck. The passenger in the car had the window down and a gun pointing at Helm. Helm pulled over as two masked men approached the truck. One of the men got behind the steering wheel and ordered Helm to get into the car that was now behind the truck. His eyes were covered and his hands tied. He was told to get down on the floorboard. The car followed the truck for about 8 1/2 hours before the truck stopped. The car stopped on a country road and dumped Helm in a weedy ditch.

After freeing his hands and eyes, Helm walked until he saw an Illinois State Police car from East St. Louis. He told the trooper what happened and the trooper returned to his headquarters to alert other districts and neighboring state police. Helm was taken to Springfield and left at the Mueller' liquor business.

One of the hijackers took Helms' truck to Paducah where a man by the name of Pearson was waiting for it. From Paducah the truck was driven to Memphis on back roads. Pearson had arranged for an International truck to be waiting outside of Memphis. The whiskey was transferred to the International truck and hauled to Risco, Missouri, about 70 miles southwest of Cairo. Somewhere between Memphis and Risco one of the men who helped to transfer the whiskey to the International truck purchased several cases knowing that it was stolen liquor. Around January 8, 1950, the Mueller truck was found in a ditch outside of Memphis."

Paul Pearson had a squeaky-clean record and was well respected as a businessman in Cairo and neighboring states for purchasing liquor in large quantities. He had covered his tracks well. In 1949, Pearson purchased nearly $180,000 worth of whiskey and other liquors from J.B. Wenger paying cash for the purchases. Records at J.B. Wingers' indicating who and how much liquor was purchased by Pearson have been lost or destroyed.

In the past, Pearson sent much of his trucks of liquor north of Cairo to Karnak, Illinois. In doing so, he was avoiding tax authorities and local police who may have remembered the license plates on the trucks that were loaded at Wenger's. It was common knowledge that some of the local police were connected to criminals that hijacked trucks.

Earlier in the year, Pearson had his drivers park Pearson's trucks behind Club Winchester, south of Olmsted, before going on to Karnak. Shot Winchester agreed upon such arrangements as long as he didn't know why they were doing this or what was in the trucks. Shot knew the local cops were aware of the hijackings and were taking a cut to leave the hijackers alone. He allowed his parking lot to serve as the liquor exchange area so that the cops would leave him alone.

On one occasion during the summer of 1949, a Mack truck pulled in behind the Club Winchester just as the sun came up. Seconds later, two Cadillac's pulled up alongside of the Mack truck. The back seats had been removed from the cars. It became apparent that the three men knew each other. The driver unlocked the side door of the truck and the three men loaded several cases of whiskey in the back of the cars. The driver accepted an envelope containing money as his share of the deal. When the transfer was complete, the truck driver shut the side door to the truck and headed north. The two cars loaded with the whiskey headed south on Route 37. Later it was believed that the driver of one of the Cadillac's was a well-known hoodlum from Cairo. The list of possible responsible parties was narrowed down because a Cadillac just wasn't seen in the area during the late 40's.

Hijackers from Missouri, Illinois, and Kentucky knew that the Cairo Liquor Company was selling whiskey illegally to bootleggers who would drive to Cairo and load up their cars. The driver, with a route memorized, headed for the southern states, and sold it for a greater amount. The city and county police knew what was going on but accepted payoffs to look the other way. By the end of 1950, Cairo had a $20 million bootlegging business.

Buster Wortman and the sultans of southern Illinois had built their own kingdoms in rum -running, bootlegging, gambling, and the various other rackets that they controlled. Dominating the southern counties with their own set of rules and punishment for decades, they had corrupted police officers, politicians, and even Governor Dwight Greene. Greene, after successfully prosecuting Al Capone, seemed to have turned soft on gambling. Since Greene's re-election in 1944, who won by gangster contributions, over one-third of the state had wide open gambling. Governor Greene was playing both sides against each other by verbally condemning gambling in public but allowing it in the Lake Club, in Springfield, Illinois that found Springfield's legislators regular customers.

Another racket that increased the revenue shared by the criminals in southern Illinois was the numbers game. The Shelton gang and Frank 'Buster' Wortman had gambling in Central and Southern Illinois wrapped up by 1945. The quest for more territory between the two would lead to Bernie Shelton's murder in Peoria, Illinois.

The Rackets

The numbers racket is more than a century old. It was organized crime's version of what we call the lottery today. People picked one or more numbers taking a chance that their number would be drawn. For many decades, the state of Florida had the biggest numbers racket due to a well-organized and established criminal element. It was primarily the unemployed or low income blacks who choose this form of gambling because it was cheap. A nickel or dime bet on a three-number combination from 000 to 999 could make all their dreams come true. On a weekend night the winning number or numbers were drawn. The game was often rigged and the 'house' usually took eight dollars out of every ten dollars wagered.

Al Capone saw little use in the numbers racket and considered it beneath him. He paid no attention to the income other mobsters were getting from it as it was a 'poor mans' game in his eyes. Chicago's attitude changed after the death of Capone and the Outfit muscled their way into the racket.

Wortman and other mobsters in southern Illinois noticed the dollar value of instituting it in their illegal businesses. They used bars, basements in private homes, abandoned buildings, and parking lots for their operation. Over a period of a few years the numbers racket was generating over $1 million a year. Number wheels that displayed the winning numbers were purchased from a Chicago based factory that was specially designed for the numbers racket. The wheel was about the size of an oil drum and had a crank-turn. The factory also delivered the wheels to the various locations where the drawings were held.

In his booze running days, Shot Winchester ran 'number slips' to East Cape Girardeau and East St. Louis for Wortman's crew. Sometimes as many as 100 slips to each place on a single trip. His drop off place in East Cape Girardeau was an abandoned car in an alley. The car was covered with coal dust except for the door handle on the driver's side. Shot would place the slips in a pitched vegetable box in the back floorboard. In East St. Louis he met a man in the residential district who took a small chicken feed bag filled with slips from him. Early the next week one of Wortman's employees would bring Shot his pay in cash.

Dice games which included craps, had a pair of dice thrown by the player in hopes of rolling a 7 or 11. If a 2, 3 or 12 turned up the house would win that bet or bets. The other numbers were termed rollovers. If not rigged it was one of the fairest games. There were numerous ways to 'rig' the dice game. A table could be manufactured with a magnet installed that forced the dice to turn up a 2, 3, or 12. The dice used in the game could be weighted with a magnet inserted to do the same thing. Some craps dealers were good at palming a 'loaded' dice and using it to guarantee a house win on a throw.

The game of roulette began in New Orleans by blacks who also made the rules for playing the game. Due to its popularity in the southern states, it traveled up the Mississippi River on steam and paddleboats during the Civil War and remained popular in towns like Cairo, Illinois. Chicago's criminals were often seen at southern Illinois clubs that had the roulette wheels and they convinced Capone to put it in his speakeasies.

Roulette was easily rigged with mechanical pins that pop up on a numbered 'slot' when the wheel is spinning. The wheel has 38 potential slots to catch a spinning ball. At the top of the table are 0 and 00, which is reserved for the house. This gives the player 36-1 odds of winning with a single bet. The house only paid out 34-1 so again, the house has a guaranteed profit.

Roulette and craps netted the crime lords hundreds of millions a year from these games around the state. Slot machines gave a good $1,200 on a weekend night to Little Egypt's sultans *after* the club owners cut.

Though cagey and coy, all the sultans of southern Illinois and even the kingpins knew that the rackets they made their fortunes on had a specific life span. The message was in the wind.

MAUREEN HUGHS

The Last Dance

In the background of gambling backers, stood a large number of Illinoisans who rebuked the wide-open corruption that gambling had brought to the state. Over one-third of Illinois had some form of gambling and the voters needed to find a candidate who would censure it and make any form illegal. Governor Greene avoided discussing it as many of his legislators frequented establishments that offered gambling. When election time came around voters looked hard for an opponent who was a mover and shaker and would reform the state. The candidate they chose was the incongruous Illinoisan Adlai Stevenson.

Stevenson, though appearing to be a studious, somber man enjoyed hobnobbing with moneyed people. When his political reputation became nation wide many years later he would be photographed with such socialites as Marshal Field's widow Ruth, publisher Alicia Guggenheim and Brooke Astor who shared Adlai's love for Dachshunds *and* whom Adlai proposed to while on a hiking trip. Nothing came of that relationship but they remained good friends.

In the late 1940's, Adlai Stevenson was a budding politician well versed on the vices in Illinois. With prodding from supporters, and angry voters the unassuming Democrat Stevenson ran a non-stop campaign for better government without the corruption it had experienced for decades. Stevenson proposed a bill to accent Congress's bill prohibiting the shipment of slot machines across state lines. Stevenson wanted to prohibit the manufacturing of slot machines in Illinois, which was where *most* of the machines were made. Illinois legislature vetoed the bill. Stevenson's next bill was to prohibit gambling in establishments that served alcohol. Again, his bill was shot down. Greene, knowing that Stevenson's anti-gambling bills had failed, ran for his third term as governor thinking it was a sure thing but lost in 1948 to Stevenson.

Stevenson, fully aware of the corruption, was committed to fulfill his campaign platform for a reformed government and people of moral conviction in public office. One of his top priorities, as Governor, was to reform the Illinois State Police force, which had grown to 500 when he took office. He wanted the State Police to be free of political influence and hired on merit *not* political ties.

Another was to rid the state of illegal gambling. Oddly enough, he had the green light from both political parties. Personally, Stevenson felt ridding the state of gambling should be left to the local law enforcement but was promptly ridiculed for 'passing the buck' and going soft on his campaign promises. Pressure from the press pushed the new governor into action. Initially he did not want to use the State Police to be the enforcer.

Whether Stevenson realized that the mafia had local mobsters in their pocket or that gambling was just a way that local government supported their town budgets is unclear. He was responding to the pressure that had been put upon him and his own moral code.

Brett Berger, whose grandfather was Captain Elza Brantly of the Illinois State Police District #13, remembers stories that his grandfather told about those years.

"At that time, a department of criminal investigation was unheard of in Illinois. The Illinois State Police was responsible for controlling all the vices as well as traffic issues. However, when Stevenson saw how entrenched the gambling was he knew it would require more than a handful of selected, deputized men. Stevenson had access to the statistics of where the establishments were and how much the state acquired in taxes from the various games," Berger said.

Captain Brantley had 104 state troopers at his disposal to cover 27 counties in southern Illinois, which included East Saint Louis. The troopers took 36 hours out of their workweek to conduct raids on various establishments that had illegal gambling and allowed prostitution in their clubs. Most of the raids, at that time, were conducted without search warrants.

Brantley wrote in his memoirs, "Troopers couldn't get search warrants because, in most cases, the States Attorney's and the County Sheriff's had been paid off by the club owners. Even the Justice of the Peace would not issue a search warrant for fear of threats or harm to them by the club owners and the gamblers.

I spent a lot of time in Alexander, Pulaski, Williamson

and Johnson Counties raiding gambling and houses of prostitution. We raided five nightclubs in Alexander County 90 straight nights. Three times a night with search warrants that I made using only one trooper at each club. The hardest hit was the Purple Club (which later became the Purple Crackle), the Colony Club, Buddy Buddy Lounge, and Club 51. There was no overtime pay given or extra days off during this time. We worked around the clock when necessary. Buster Wortman had full ownership of slot and pinball machines and horse parlors in southern Illinois counties by the late 1940's. The biggest raid was at the Fireworks Station in East St. Louis. Buster was present at the raid and ditched his .32 Cal. pistol under a curtain when he ran out."

May 1950, from the top of the state to Cairo in Alexander County chosen troopers of the Illinois State Police force conducted the secret raids. Not one slot machine, dice table, horse racing results wallboard, or roulette wheel was spared being removed from the premises that had the gambling equipment or the demolition of the equipment by the troopers. It should be understood that Governor Stevenson did not want warrants made out on owners or operators of the businesses with gambling within but on the slot machines and tables in the establishments. Slot machines and pinball machines were taken to the respective county state's attorney's office to be logged and labeled 'property of the state of Illinois'.

One resident of Cairo stated that Jake Rubin had advanced warning that his club was to be raided. When the state police came through the door, they looked around the bare floor of the club. Rubin, standing behind the bar was grinning at the cops.

"We have a warrant to confiscate your slot machines Mr. Rubin. Where are they? The cop asked. Jake Rubin took the warrant from the cop, read it, and started laughing. He led the officers to the Cache River some distance from his club. There, behind a tree along the riverbank were his slot machines.

"Just not your day is it fellas'? Seems to me you are just out of luck. This warrant states *within* club property. Doesn't say anything about the river bank!" Rubin said with a smirk. The state police officers swore under their breath, climbed up the riverbank and left.

A few years later Jake Rubin would buy another honky tonk and name it Latin Quarters. Rubin had one of the first stereo systems installed in the plush club and used the small building next to the club for his gambling operation.

It was common for the clubs to have only one door. Rubin's club had an entrance door reinforced with ¼-inch steel between the outer and inner parts of the door. This was to prevent the cops from busting through as they usually did unannounced. In the 1960's, Jake Rubin would be murdered in his own club. Witnesses were all around when the murder occurred but when they were summoned to testify they stated that *they* hadn't seen or heard anything.

The state police left no club behind in the raids. Capt. Brantley led a raid at the Thunderbird club shortly after Rubin's club, which netted dice and blackjack tables and the arrest of eight men including the local Justice of the Peace, O.R. Clark of Thebes, Illinois. Elmer Terrell of Mounds, Illinois was arrested for operating a gambling establishment when his Frog City club was raided. His Peoria, Illinois attorney, Joseph C. Sudow, stated that the club was incorporated but would not identify the officers. Brantley checked county records and found that the corporation was not listed in any of the Alexander County Circuit Court records. Also, *not registered* were the financial backers of the club. Alexander County seemed to be notorious for that. Michael O'Shea, Alexander County State's Attorney assured Brantley he would look into whether a violation had occurred.

It was common for Brantley to send plain clothes officers into a club to see what type of gambling was going on. Sometimes they would go more than once and then report to Brantley who would then get a warrant and raid the establishment. This happened at the El Patio, owned by Jake Rubin in the winter of 1956.The raid occurred at 11:30 pm and netted card tables, slot machines and other gambling devices. Ralph Brown was arrested and fined $100.Others involved were from either Cairo or towns in Kentucky.

Following the El Patio raid, Brantley's State Troopers raided the Thunderbird club and arrested eight men for operating a gambling establishment and participating in the games. All the gambling equipment was taken from the club and stored as evidence at District 13 headquarters.

Captain Brantley's gambling raids included clubs and taverns that dealt only in the numbers racket. It was commonly referred to as the "Policy Game." One raid was at the Fireworks Station in the East St. Louis district. The tavern was taking in over $200 a week. His biggest raid netting the most money with the most patrons was the Corona Club. Buster Wortman was one of the patrons who attempted to escape being arrested. He was charged and fined but did manage to throw his 9 millimeter Browning automatic pistol away and escaped a gun charge.

Shot's Club Winchester was not spared being raided. Archie Slagle remembers the night Brantley's troopers crashed through the door of the Club Winchester.

"It was a good night. Many people dining and dancing. The craps table had people lined up two deep and the roulette table was busy. Very few slot machines were inactive and lots of laughter was coming from the black jack table. The state police was carrying hatchets when they entered. It was sickening to see what the troopers did. I was standing next to Shot when the hatchets came down on the tables. They cut them in half and then smashed them so they were irreparable. With every hit, I could hear Shot groan. He had the prettiest tables this side of the Mississippi River! It was awful. The slot machines were smashed and carried out along with the tables...just pieces of wood now. They took the chips and all the cash that was there. In other raids, I had heard that the equipment was just removed. Maybe broken down to fit through the doors but not smashed up as they did at Club Winchester. I know they were just doing their job but it seemed to be a vendetta against Shot.

The state police had moving vans to haul the equipment away. It was often joked that the club owners had Brown Moving Company bring in the gambling tables, wheels, and slot machines in to the clubs and the police retained the same company to haul the broken equipment out! It was a funny sight."

After the court hearings gambling tables that served as evidence were burnt, usually in the county they were confiscated in. In the early raids, slot machines were inventoried and stored in a warehouse. Stevenson knew that East coast crime families would bribe the East coast warehouse owners, buy the machines, and re-establish them in *their* gambling houses. He vowed that that would not happen in Illinois and had the machines smashed to unusable pieces. All in all $20,000 worth of gambling equipment was confiscated from Pulaski County alone.

Along with Adlai Stevenson, a little known freshman senator from Tennessee, Estes Kefauver, well versed on organized crime was appointed chairman of the U. S. Senate Special Committee on Interstate Commerce crime within organized crime. In 1950, Kefauver had the senate hearings on organized crime moved from Miami to New York State making interstate gambling his platform. Kefauver became very vocal on the subject both to satisfy his Southern Baptist upbringing and his political aspirations.

What Kefauver did not take into consideration was the mobsters were immigrants or children of immigrants who wanted to become respected citizens and secure a marked place in the American life they had heard about. Because of their immigrant status or accents, they felt this was the only way they could make a mark in the business world. They used this argument in court and stated that they were being harassed. Kefauver refused to make the distinction between the weekend gambler and the organized criminal and went after all of them.

Kefauver's approach, an all-out, nationwide investigation, scared the criminal element. Among themselves, the mafia talked of spanning out to untouched territories and even out of the country to avoid being investigated. In the U.S. the urgency of Kefauver's plea was somewhat ignored by the government until two gangsters from the Chicago Outfit were murdered in Kansas City, Missouri in 1950. *Then* Congress could no longer bury the bills Estes Kefauver presented and made organized crime a top priority. Some of the mafia leaders scoffed at the senate hearings saying Kefauver wasn't much better than they were. To some degree, they were right. Estes Kefauvfer had accepted campaign contributions from a numbers racketeer in his hometown state.

During these turbulent times, making the newspapers every day, Shot realized the prognosis. Business was down and the raids continued scaring *more* people away. It was harder to contract entertainment and when he did, paying them was harder as there was no gambling revenue coming in. He would have to sell his club.

In late 1952 Charles E. Witt and his wife, Betty, who owned a hotel in Decatur, Illinois purchased the mahogany bar and beveled mirrors with Shot's dogs etched in them. Both he and his wife had been to Club Winchester many times, loved the elegance of the bar, and wanted to place the bar pieces in their hotel.

The Sinclair Oil Company purchased the building with the intention of storing bulk fuel on the main floor. The oil company paid Shot Winchester $40,000 for the entire building; very different from what Shot had invested in it. However, the gambling days were over so he took what he could get out of it. All the employees found jobs elsewhere in the area or in St. Louis.

For some unknown reason Sinclair Oil never used the building. Years later, it was re-sold to Homer Fergeson Sr. to be converted into an aluminum storm door and window plant.

In 1953, Shot Winchester opened Club 37 on the north edge of the 12 acres he had purchased years ago for Club Winchester. Club 37 was much smaller and far less extravagant and sat parallel to Route 37. Shot used a room in the northwest corner of the club to sleep in when working late into the night. He had a small 30'X30' building built behind Club 37 for himself after bar hours closed. To obtain a liquor license, Shot put the Club 37 liquor license in LaVera Mae Ford's name. She lived with Shot in the building behind Club 37.

Paul Powell, the up and coming Illinois politician and close friend to Shot, tried to convince him to open a bar in Carbondale, Illinois. It was a college town and Paul thought Shot would do well there financially. Shot was not excited with the picture Paul painted. He felt he had clientele that would support his smaller club and he would be able to support himself and family.

Archie Slagle said of Club 37, "Florence and I moved back to Olmsted in 1952. Shot asked me to stay with him and work there. I was happy to do so. I found Shot easy to work for. He was a good boss. Shot wanted me to put the floor in the new club and sent me to Paducah first to buy what I needed. I went to all the flooring stores and then all over creation looking for floor tiles. I would buy up remnants and pieces that had been discontinued for almost nothing. I brought them back to the club and figured out a design that I could use all of them and did! It was unique and looked really good!

Sometimes Shot would ask me how much money I needed for pay. I was doing fine on the $51 he paid me at Club Winchester so my pay remained the same. I was paid cash every week. No bookkeeping and no taxes. Guess the both of us could have gotten into trouble with that. The club was nice and welcoming but what a change from Club Winchester! People came in with their work clothes on. They sometimes brought their children if they were there just for a couple of beers. There wasn't linen table clothes on the tables and the bartender looked like a customer. No white jackets and no spit polished shoes. Shot still had his flower garden and did have flowers in the club sometimes. The entertainment was a jukebox not the big name bands, orchestras or comedy acts...just a little box you dropped nickels into and picked a song to be played. However, Shot made it fun to work there and everybody seemed to be happy when they were in the new club.

In '54, I worked weekends at Club 37 and got a full time job at the Old Opera House in East Cape Girardeau, Missouri. *That* was a nightclub on the level that the Club Winchester had been. The pay was good and full time work was even better. After about a year in Cape Girardeau I did less work for Shot. His business was good but he could handle most of the weekend customers himself. Florence and I would still have Shot up for supper a lot. Florence use to say if it wasn't for her Shot wouldn't eat! He was always working."

On a few occasions, Shot allowed trucks to park behind the old Club Winchester building as long as he did not know who the driver was, what was in the trucks, or whom they were hiding from. By doing so, he was out of the loop of hijackers and it helped to ensure the law enforcement people, who may be on the take, to leave him alone."

Hijacking remained a profitable business for both the local mobsters and those that controlled them. In 1941, the mafia and its sub-groups had gained control of the transport unions. Hijacking trucks heading for Chicago and St. Louis became almost commonplace. Shot knew the drivers were using Illinois Route 37 to avoid state police patrols on major highways.

Adlai Stevenson's pressure on gambling and other rackets caused mob leaders to force other mobsters out of the slot machine racket. Estes Kefauver's committee against organized crime threatened the livelihood of the hoodlums in Cairo. This was especially true when newspapers printed stories about the $20 million bootlegging business in Cairo, Illinois. The local hoodlums were intimidated and nervous about how to keep their rackets going and not get caught.

Sometime during 1955, Shot was to accept a truck loaded with sugar. The sugar had been paid for in advance by Shot and was to be delivered to his parking lot. Shot *thought* he had purchased it on the market and would resell for a higher price in either Missouri or Kentucky. The deal was phony, the money taken and no sugar arrived. A few people who wanted Shot to lose his business and had hopes of driving him away began to concoct stories of what had happened. Rumors started around Alexander and Pulaski Counties that Shot had received *stolen* sugar and had sold it *or* was hiding it somewhere. The rumors were believed by local law enforcement. The situation became well known in Cairo and would be used against Shot in a few months by Pulaski County Sheriff, Bob Aldridge. Whether Sheriff Aldridge *knew* the arrangement was phony from the start *or* part of it was never admitted to in any of the interviews. Sheriff Aldridge did publically swear, "He would get Winchester!"

Early in July of 1955, Shot Winchester was formally indicted on nine counts of receiving stolen property. The indictment didn't specify what stolen property he had and left many people wondering if Pulaski County Sheriff, Robert Aldridge was using the rumors to indict Winchester. He was free on a $9,000 bond. This left Shot bitter and angry with Sheriff Robert Aldridge as Shot's testimony seemed to be ignored during the hearing.

MAUREEN HUGHS

The Tin Inn Murder

Club 37 and the Tin Inn were only about a mile apart on Route 37. One would have to drive several miles before coming to another bar. Shot Winchester was well acquainted with Clate Adams, owner of the Tin Inn.

Archie Slagle said of the relationship between the two bar owners. "There were times when the two of them would shoot the breeze over a coke and beer at one or the other's bar. They were friends and mostly just talked business or the recent robberies to area clubs. Sometimes they would joke about who had the best dogs. Shot had the hunting dogs that were well known in the area and the Clate and Rosie Adams had a huge Great Dane they used for a watchdog. The size alone of that sucker would intimidate anyone! Both Shot and Clate had been hurt business-wise with the gambling raids conducted by the State Police but had hung on for the most part. They didn't need to compete with one another. They each had their own crowds that patronized their clubs. Clate was a year or so older than Shot and had previously owned a tavern in Metropolis I believe. I don't know why he left Metropolis or if he built the Tin Inn. I just remember the robbery gone bad that took place there. It was a terrible thing that happened."

During the evening of February 23, 1956, Norman R. Halliday Jr. age 33, of Cairo, Illinois and Alfred Leroy Reahm, age 37 who also went by Al Masters from Cairo, stopped at a gas station in Cairo to fill Halliday's car. From Cairo they drove north on highway 37 and stopped at Club 37. Shot had the TV on when the men entered so they sat at the bar.

After drinking a few beers and talking among themselves, they struck up a conversation with Shot that included robbing taverns. One of the men asked if Shot had been robbed. Thinking the beers they had drank caused them to start talking stupid. Shot ignored the question. While washing the last of the glasses and sweeping the floor behind the bar they again, asked about robbing the club. Shot jokingly said they should go to the Tin Inn if they wanted to rob a place." The owner of the Tin Inn has more money than I do *now!* Shot said sarcastically while thinking of the nine thousand dollar he had to fork over to bond out of jail.

After another beer the two men left club 37 and went North on Route 37 towards the Tin Inn. It was 10:30pm.

The parking lot to the Tin Inn was empty as the two men circled the bar. Parking the car at the far end of the parking lot, they walked in. Looking around they walked to the bar ordered a pack of cigarettes and two beers. Clate and his wife were by themselves that night; their son, Steve, was on a safari in Africa with friends.

While the two men watched TV Adam's 200 pound Great Dane sauntered into the bar section heading towards the living quarters of the Tin Inn. Seeing the dog Halliday and Reahm talked about having a dog and which breed was better than another. As it was drawing close to closing time, Rosie Adams went behind the bar and turned off the TV. This seemed to irritate the men. "Why did you do that?" One of them asked. Rosie explained that due to the hour the local station would cease programs for the night. Telling her husband that she was turning in, Rosie followed their dog to the living quarters in the northeast corner of the tavern.

Clate Adams informed the men that he was closing up for the night when Reahm said, "We'll need a half pint of whiskey for the road." When Adams brought the bottle of whiskey from under the bar, Reahm pointed a .45 pistol at his face. Adams, trying not to act concerned waved the gun away and asked Reahm what he wanted suspecting a robbery was about to happen. Pretending to ignore the situation Adams turned toward the living quarters to get his gun when Reahm fired the first shot hitting Adams in the stomach. Adams fell to the floor but attempted to keep crawling to where his gun was.

As she got into bed, Rosie heard gunfire. Running back to the bar she heard Clate yell for her to get his gun. When Rosie got to the bar entrance Reahm leaned over the bar and fired a second shot into Adams' back. Rosie screamed and the Great Dane entered the bar and immediately shot to death by Reahm who turned and fired at Rosie, narrowly missing her. She reached for the phone to call the police. Clate, still crawling, reached for his gun. He turned and fired once missing both men. Reahm them fired the third and fatal shot into Adams' back. As the two men headed for the door they fired back into the bar again just missing Rosie Adams as she was talking to the police.

Leaving the bar, Reahm fired one more bullet through the window of the Tin Inn and got into the car. One of the men reloaded the gun while they drove south to a small community called America just off highway 37. There they threw the .45 gun out the window forgetting they had reloaded it. Zigzagging on back roads, they passed Mound City to Route 3. Feeling safe, they headed south to Cairo.

Halliday dropped Reahm off at his apartment above the Hub tavern in Cairo and he went to his home.

About 2am Friday, Frank Clifford, special investigator to Cairo's Mayor Paul Baur, was on the crime scene. After three hours of talking to Rosie Adams and picking up spent shells and other bits of evidence, Clifford had enough information to determine who the men were. Later that day highway workers cleaning trash from the roadside found the gun. Investigator Clifford identified it as the same gun that had been stolen from Reahm weeks earlier. Investigator Clifford, who later found the gun, recorded the gun's serial number and returned it to Reahm. Through ballistic tests, Investigator Clifford confirmed that the gun found outside of America, was the murder weapon. Clifford, Cairo Police Sergeant William Hastings, and State Trooper Don Evers surrounded Reahm's apartment above the Hub tavern. Reahm quietly surrendered when confronted by officers.

Norman Halliday was arrested in his home and a .45 automatic was found belonging to Halliday.

Halliday and Reahm were charged with the murder of Clate Adams on February 27, 1956. Norman Halliday, represented by Joe Crain of Mound City and John Crain of Cairo, signed a formal confession, blamed the shooting on Al Reahm. Halliday said Reahm had wanted to "hit the Tin Inn because he had heard that Adams had $12,000hidden in the tavern."

Further, in his confession Halliday stated that he and Reahm had another set of clothes in the car to change after the robbery. "I thought we were *just* going to rob the place. We brought the extra clothes to change into after we robbed them. After the shooting we headed for America where we got out of the car, changed clothes, and threw the other clothes away." This proved to be a lie when the clothes were found in Halliday's car trunk. Alfred Reahm would later attempt to kill Halliday and was transferred to Statesville prison in upstate Illinois.

Local authorities checked both men for outstanding warrants. The results found that Alfred Reahm had a previous criminal record and was currently wanted in Brownsville, Texas on a forgery charge. He had been in Cairo for a few weeks. How the two men met is unclear.

At his grand Jury hearing, shortly after the Clate Adams' murder, Reahm was asked why he and Halliday chose the Tin Inn to rob. Reahm looked to Clifford and Sheriff Aldrich sitting in the grand jury and said that Lester (Shot) Winchester was involved in the case. When asked how this could be Reahm stated," We were at Shot's club first on Route 37 and had a couple of beers there. Norman and I joked about robbing Shot's tavern and he told us to go to the Tin Inn as Clate Adams had $12,000 hidden somewhere in the tavern."

Hearing this Sheriff Aldrich jump up and hit the table he was sitting at with his fist saying, "I knew the bastard was dirty! I just *knew* it!" The judge ordered silence in the courtroom and asked Aldrich to sit down.

Alfred Reahm knew how much Aldrich hated Winchester and if it would take some years off his sentence... what the hell, tell them anything! Reahm knew he did not tell the true story of what Winchester had actually said to the two of them while they were in Club 37 but thought the Grand Jury might go easier on him thinking there was more than just himself and Halliday involved. Both men were ordered held over for trial later.

Alfred Reahm had been sitting in a Metropolis bar two seats away from Clate Adams and a friend of his when Clate talked about not disclosing all his earnings for the previous year. Two nights prior to the Adams murder, Reahm heard Clate state that he had some $12,000 hid away to start the New Year. Reahm left the bar shortly after that to start plotting how *he* could get that money.

After the arraignment of Reahm and Halliday, Cairo Police Chief Robert Aldrich left the courthouse in a hurry. He had a lot to think over. It looked like he would have enough evidence to hang Shot Winchester with the new implication that he was involved with the Clate Adams murder. But, Alfred Reahms was a seasoned criminal and knew all the ropes and angles. Aldridge wasn't sure that when the two men went to trial the jury would believe Reahms' allegation about Shot's involvement. Moreover, a newer issue that he *knew* Shot was aware of was going on. Would Shot testify to what he knew about *him* and the others? Did Shot know all the people involved in the new *business* he and the others were in? Aldrich could not relax. He had a lot to consider and plans made to sweep the truth under the rug for fear of being caught.

A few days later, after talking with his attorney, Alfred Reahm pleaded guilty to murder, waived his right to a trial by jury, and was sentenced to 180 years by Judge C. Ross Reynolds of Vienna, Illinois. His record was sealed for 75 years and is as yet unavailable.

MAUREEN HUGHS

Follow the Money

The 1950's brought indictments for mafia and mob leaders across the East coast and beyond. Little Egypt was no exception. Crime was boiling over in southern Illinois. Estes Kefauver's senate hearings had put the fear of God in the most fearless. Many Mafia leaders had moved to unclaimed territories to avoid summons to testify before Kefauver. The West coast was the place to go to hide out until the heat was off while the underlings in the various crime families took the rap for the leaders. Southern Illinois was not affected immediately but sensed the trouble that *could* head their way.

The Senate Committee on Interstate Commerce Crime could not have come at a worse time. Santo Trafficante Sr. had full control of the crime in Tampa Florida. He had groomed his son to take over so he could focus on increasing his power in Cuba. His goal was to put Cuba under his control with the casino business though he did not live long enough for that to happen. Neither Trafficante men had any reservations about getting into the narcotics business. They were one of the first crime families in the United States to do so.

Carlo Marcello, though not in full control of New Orleans until the early 1960's, had a great deal of political pull and was well entrenched in a market that mafia family leaders fervently publicly denied...narcotics!

The Sicilian Mafia had long been involved in the drug business. For fifty years, they were the top supplier of heroin on an international basis making millions in both the heroin and cocaine market. The Sicilians saw their chance to gain even more by expanding their ground in America. The American Mafia for decades denied being involved in the illegal drug business. The leaders of the five families on the East coast felt it was a disgusting business and beneath them. They were doing just fine with the rackets they controlled. Joe Bonanno made it a 'family' rule to stay out of the business but when he found some of his men had broken this rule he had no problem accepting money received from narcotics.

It was not long before Joe Bonanno saw how lucrative the drug business was for the Sicilian mob and gradually implemented it into one of his businesses. Charles Luciano had been quietly arranging a narcotics deal with the Sicilians. By the end of the 1950, the American and Sicilian Mafias were in bed with each other over narcotics. Bonanno's decision to be involved in narcotics didn't just affect his crime family or the families along the East coast. It changed things for the entire United States.

In 1954 or 1955, Bonanno, always looking to increase his control and wealth arranged a meeting with the Canadian crime boss, Victor Cotroni, for the sole purpose of enhancing his power and territory. Since narcotics were coming into American through Canada, Bonanno wasn't going to let an opportunity pass him by. Having some control over the Canadian drug traffic into the states, Bonanno was building a broader network throughout the United States.

At the same time that Joe Bonanno was increasing his empire with narcotics coming into New York from Sicily and now Canada, other mob bosses in the southern states were forging relationships with Cuba, Haiti, and Mexico for the same purpose.

The Herrera crime family in Mexico had been the major heroin distributor in the 1950's. They too, wanted to expand their pipeline into the states, as did Cuba and corrupt politicians in Haiti.

Trafficante was dealing with Guatemala's narcotic lords and selling cigars back to them from his cigar sweatshops. Marcello was networking with Cuba and Mexico to bring their narcotics into New Orleans.

When the rewards of such a venture were received in Chicago, the Outfit desperately wanted a piece of the action. They had already, silently, been in the narcotics business since the end of WWII and had limited connections with the Canadian mob dealing in narcotics. Connected to East St. Louis and southern Illinois mobsters reduced expenses, gave a quicker delivery time, and offered unlimited revenue.

Cairo, Illinois was the unassuming town that met the criteria to bring in skimmed money off gambling in Cuba and Mexico. Money from prostitution, loan sharks, and now narcotics could be distributed in banks or stored in businesses fronted by the St. Louis and Chicago crime families and associates. Nightclubs, bars, warehouses, and local business in Cairo and surrounding communities served as storage areas for the money until arrangements could be made to get the money out of state and often out of the country. The money was then used to start new business elsewhere and, of course, payoffs. Money from these illegal enterprises were transported up from Miami, Tampa, and New Orleans to Memphis and on to Cairo, Illinois.

Tony Giordano, the up and coming St. Louis mobster, served as the prime drug courier for the St. Louis family. Cairo became the stopping off place for laundered money to be picked up and drugs dropped off prior to continuing on to Memphis. When not serving as courier he worked in the vending machine racket until he was convicted on income tax charges in 1956.

Shot knew that drugs were coming into Alexander and Pulaski Counties. Cairo became the hub for drug circulation throughout the country. He had no part in the concealing or circulation of it but knew which sultans of Little Egypt did. *All* of them. Moreover, he knew a certain amount of law enforcement officers and politicians collected their graft from it by keeping quiet. Shot Winchester didn't pay much attention to what was happening. He did not agree with it and was not involved in any way. But he *knew!*

Pulaski County Sheriff, Robert Aldrich was concerned with how to handle Winchester's knowledge. He could see the threat of what Shot could do if he went to trial over the stolen property indictment. He would use his knowledge of narcotics coming into Cairo as an advantage for the charges. He could also talk to the FBI and cause many people to lose their county jobs and income. Sheriff Aldrich also took into consideration that Reahm, who indicated that Shot Winchester was involved in the Clate Adams murder, wasn't a man to trust. Reahm was out for himself and whatever it took to get a reduced sentence. Aldrich decided to speak to people who could help come up with a way to silence Winchester and keep the truth from being told. *He* had too much to lose!

By mid-March of 1956, Aldrich had spoken with people who were getting pay offs from the narcotics deals that were centered in Cairo. One person was Bill Harris, a former convict and friend of Shot Winchester. Shot had employed Harris shortly after Harris was placed on parole. Shot felt that Bill Harris had done his time and gone straight. With a decent job, he could support his himself and his wife, Peggy. Shot also let Harris stay in one of the apartments he had built behind the Club Winchester that had been used for employees at times. Shot wasn't aware that Harris was involved in the narcotics deals up to his eyeballs. Harris was one of the transporters! Harris agreed to help Aldrich and the others cook up a way of eliminating the threat of Shot going to the authorities. "Leave it to me," Harris said. Aldrich did. Sheriff Aldrich could see how this would work in his favor. Let Harris work out a plan and if Shot *did* talk to the authorities they would look at Bill Harris's record, know that he was a convict and think he was implicating Aldridge to help himself.

Kenneth S. of Tennessee recalls how the plans were laid for Shot Winchester's murder. "Over the next several days Shot noticed a change in Bill Harris. He would tell Shot he couldn't work on some days and then wouldn't leave Shot's side on other days. He would offer to do work for Shot or pick up supplies for him in Metropolis or wherever Shot had ordered supplies and liquor at. Days before Shot was killed, Harris asked Shot to go with him to Paducah, Kentucky to buy a gun. Shot wanted to know why Harris was so damn set on getting a gun! Harris explained that with the recent robberies at the bars and taverns, he would feel more secure with one when he worked.

Shot was with Harris when he purchased a .38 pistol from a sporting goods store in Paducah, April 2, 1956. Harris used the alias William Smith of Fulton, Kentucky as *he* couldn't openly buy a weapon due to his criminal record and Shot couldn't for the same reason. Back then, they didn't have computers to check a person's criminal record nor did buyers have to wait three days to actually remove the gun from the gun shop.

They returned to Club 37 where Harris put the gun in his apartment. Off and on Sheriff Aldridge would come by the club looking for Shot. Sometimes Aldridge was alone and sometimes he brought another officer or two or a county deputy with him. He actually had a fear of Shot. I'm not sure why but Aldridge knew Shot was a hunter and good with weapons. Shot would disappear when he saw Aldrich pull into the driveway. He was not about to go back to jail. He told friends this and I believed him. He knew he had played no part in the Adams murder and he knew Aldrich *knew* he didn't. This was just Bob...trying to be a big shot! You see, Bob Aldrich couldn't resist making money, even if it was dirty. Shot on the other hand made his money the honest way...hard work. Aldridge had always had it in for Shot. He had bragged to people how he was going to get Shot and if he failed or if Shot told the authorities, what he knew then Bob would look stupid and probably not get elected sheriff again.

Sometime later, maybe a day or so, Harris called Shot at the club and said he wanted to meet with him after Shot closed the club for the night. Said he had something to tell him. Shot wanted him to come to the club and they could talk there but Harris wouldn't do it...said he meet him on old Route 37 by the maintenance driveway and they could talk then."

(At the inquest, Bill Harris told a different story saying he had closed up that night. According to Gregory S., Shot closed up the club. Harris was at his apartment with his wife, Peggy, until he left to meet Shot.)

Gregory S. continues, "Shot knew something was up. He had heard rumors that someone from Vienna, Illinois would be waiting to get him. Maybe Bill Harris knew who *they* were and had a lead on when they were coming. He agreed to meet with Harris that night. About 8pm, Shot called his wife, Izzy, who was living in Rosiclare. He asked her to meet him at the club and told his wife that a murder indictment had been issued against him over the Clate Adams killing. Izzy drove down to Club 37 and tried to get Shot to return to Rosiclare with her. Shot wouldn't go as Sheriff Bob Aldrich was looking for him and someone was hunting him in Vienna. Shot knew that if Aldrich and the others found him they would take his personal possessions so he gave $800 in cash to her. He then took off his Elks club ring that had either a .50 or.75 caret diamond in it. On his other hand, he wore a platinum band with 3.78

cart diamond in it. He slipped it off and gave both rings to Izzy. He kept his wristwatch and billfold. Shot told Izzy to go back home and wait for him. Izzy again tried to persuade Shot to return to Rosiclare with her but he refused saying, "If I go back there, they will get me. I'll kill myself before I go back to jail again."

The Set Up

Around 2:30am, April 7, 1956, nightclub owner, Shot Winchester, drove by his *Club 37*, for what would be his last time. Shot was to meet Bill Harris who had said he could help Shot and keep him out of prison. They agreed to meet by the maintenance-building driveway. Shot's new 1956 blue and white Oldsmobile was traveling on old Route 37 two miles south of Olmsted. He drove slowly down the concrete road. Oak, maple, and ash trees cast eerie shadows on the road. Shot turned off his headlights and lit an unfiltered Camel cigarette as he crept down the winding road. He stopped just beyond the state highway maintenance building and backed into the drive, leaving the car engine running. He waited. Nothing. No one around. Finishing the cigarette, he turned back north, drove to the edge of a thicket of trees and waited. A few minutes later, he turned the car around in the road using the moonlight shifting through the trees to guide his way. He rolled the driver's window down to let the cool morning air in. He was nervous. Again, he slowed down at

the highway maintenance driveway and looked around. Nothing. Just the *chirp, chirp* of a few crickets coming out of hibernation and the steady hum of his car engine.

Headlights were coming from the north on the new Route 37 and then disappeared. He had to keep moving. Again turning north, he met a car and slowly passed it. When the car was out of sight, he applied the brakes and waited a few minutes. No one around. Making a U-turn in the road he, again headed south. *Where was he?* Shot drove to the end of old Route 37, waited and listened. Nothing. Turning around and heading back north, he went to the far north end of the old road, turned around and waited several minutes. He thought Harris wasn't coming but decided to make one more pass on the road. Just north of the maintenance driveway, Shot saw the figure of a man on his left, waving his arm. The man approached out of the trees. Shot stopped the car. It was Bill Harris.

"What took you so long Bill?" Shot asked as he put the gearshift in park and left the engine running.

"Shot, I talked to Bob Aldridge. They just want to talk to you...ask you a couple of questions...that's all." Bill Harris said as he leaned against the Oldsmobile.

"Bob wants more than that Bill. He wants to hang this on *me*! He hates me enough to haul me in and...why are you shaking Bill?"

"Shot, they just want to talk to you, I swear.

"Who is *they* Bill? You keep saying *they*?"

"You know...Bob and..."

Bill Harris never finished the sentence. He stood up straight and stepped away from the car as Jake Rubin approached the Oldsmobile. Rubin stood there a moment with his hands in his coat pockets. Taking a step closer Rubin reached for the car door handle.

"Push over so we can talk Winchester. Get in the back, Bill." Shot moved to the middle of the car as Jake Rubin got in and put his gloved hands on the steering wheel.

"Bob says we have a problem with this Realm's thing. Bob thinks you will talk about some things to the Feds that he doesn't want out."

"I'm not saying a god damn thing. To you or anyone else." Shot said.

"That's not the way Bob see's it. He's got too much to lose here. He can't take any chances if the Feds put pressure on you."

Looking past Rubin, Shot saw Bill Harris look out the passenger side, curse, and get out of the car. Sensing something wasn't right Shot looked out the car's passenger window and saw a man's silhouette in the gray morning light standing on the shoulder of the road. It was Art Garner. His left hand hung to his side. His right hand held something against his leg. Shot looked back at Harris standing on the side of the road.

"What have you done, Bill?" Shot knew then it was a set up. Turning so his back was to the car door, Rubin said, "We have to solve this problem Shot…now. For everyone's sake."

Rubin got out of the car and held the door closed as the man on the right side of the car came closer. While Shot leaned over to the passenger side window, Rubin drew his gun and fired hitting the back window. Shot turned to look at Rubin who fired and missed again. Garner called out to Shot. Shot looked towards the passenger window as gunfire came from the right side of the car. Winchester fell back, then sideways in the seat. The thud of muffled bullets and shattered glass was forever held in the trees along old Route 37. A car eased its way north. Two men got in and the car continued out of sight.

Shortly after 5am, April 7, E.W. Dennis led his milk cow from the barn over the knoll to graze in the pasture. Looking through the trees on old Route 37, he noticed a car head first into the cinder pile by the maintenance driveway. He stopped to look at it and figured someone was sleeping from a night of boozing. He could hear the engine running. He went on. Walking back home he again, saw the car hadn't moved. He walked over to it. As he approached the car, he could hear the radio. Seeing the driver's window was rolled down, he looked in and saw Shot Winchester lying face down in the front seat in a pool of blood. A .38 gun lay under back under the steering wheel and close to the emergency pedal . E.W. Dennis hurried back home and called Sheriff Robert (Bob) Aldrich.

About 6am, Pulaski County Sheriff Robert Aldridge arrived at the crime scene, roped off the immediate area around the car, and supposedly stationed Mounds Police Chief, Bob Jones, Mounds City Police Chief, Leonard Hale, and Deputy John Motley at the scene. Sheriff Robert Aldridge left to call in Special State Investigator, Frank Clifford from Club 37. He also summoned a team of state criminal experts to participate in the investigation. Mr. Bode, a local photographer, was requested to take a series of pictures of the car and position of Shot Winchester *before* he was removed. An ambulance took the mortally wounded man to St. Mary's hospital in Cairo. State Trooper Don Evers and friend of Shot Winchester, arrived after Shot had been removed from the car.

About 7am, less than 24 hours after he was indicted on aiding in the death of Clate Adams, Shot Winchester was wheeled into the emergency room at St. Mary's hospital in Cairo, Illinois with a bullet wound to his head. Shot Winchester, 59 years old, was clinging to life. Past the group of people and cops that had gathered behind the stretcher that carried the mortally wounded Winchester, Sheriff Bob Aldridge hastily closed the emergency doors. Turning with his back to the emergency room doors he proudly said, "We got him boys. We finally got the son of a bitch!"

Dr. Alphonsa L. Robinson was called in to administer medical treatment on Shot. Dr. Robinson, a former native of New York, graduated from Howard University in Washington D.C. with a medical degree. After serving as a Commissioned Lieutenant in the Army Reserve, he completed his Residency in Pathology in St. Louis, Missouri. He later moved to Mounds, Illinois in 1939 and took the position of Chief of Staff at St. Mary's Hospital in Cairo.

Pete Huddleston, a grocery store owner in Olmsted had heard about the shooting and immediately called Shot's friend, Archie Slagle. Archie and Shot's wife, Izzy, drove to the hospital joining the others in the waiting room outside the Emergency room.

After a preliminary examination, Dr. Robinson went to the waiting room to speak to Izzy. "I need volunteers to give blood Mrs. Winchester. Mr. Winchester is alive but I will need blood for the surgery." As Dr. Robinson went back into the emergency room, Sheriff Aldrich cornered him just inside the doors. An argument started between the two men. Sheriff Aldrich was heard saying, "No blood. I want this over quickly. I'm warning you!"

Minutes later, Dr. Robinson again came into the waiting room and stated that blood was not needed and quickly returned to do what he could for Shot. Some 7 hours later, Lester 'Shot' Winchester was dead.

Dr. Robinson performed the autopsy. No witnesses attended to scrutinize the procedure. He had been told to complete the procedure quickly and rule the death a suicide. Dr. Robinson did verbally state to a co-worker that there was no gun residue on Shot's fingers and that it would have been almost impossible to commit suicide by firing the gun at an angle that the bullet penetrated his head. The .38 bullet should have been straight into the skull, not the area of his head above the right ear. The way this *could* have happened would be someone *else* was holding the gun and Mr. Winchester turned his head to avoid it.

It was reported that three shots were fired. One bullet through the passenger window, one though the back window on the right and one bullet that lodged in Shot's head. The bullet removed from Shot was too damaged for ballistics to determine if it was from the gun found in the car. The other two were never spoke of again. *It should be remembered that this would later be ruled a suicide.*

The Inquest

April 13, 1956 the inquest into the death of Shot Winchester was held at the Alexander County Court House, Cairo, Illinois at 7PM. Dan A. Sullivan, C.F. Walker, Charles H. Simmons, Dee Dorsett, Louis c. Johnson and William Z. Hastings sat on the inquest jury. Several witnesses were called to testify at the inquest. The inquest was conducted as follow.

Alexander County, Coroner Paul Baur, questioned the first witness.

Q. "Mr. Otto Bierbaum please state where you live and where you work."
A. "I live in Olmsted and work as a bartender for Mr. Winchester."

Q. "Mr. Bierbaum how long have you worked for him?"
A. "A little over three months."

Q. "Where you working the night of April 7th 1956?"
A. "Yes."

Q. "What time of the day do you go to work?"
A. "8:00 in the morning."

Q. "When you were working that day did you have the occasion to see Mr. Winchester and if so what time was that?"
A. "I saw him around 9:00am when he came out of the bedroom."

Q. "After he got there how long a time did he stay?"
A. "He asked me how much beer I needed. I told him and he brung it in and I put it in the box and I walked to the kitchen and I seen the car was gone.

Q. "Would that have been Mr. Winchester's car? And was he gone also?"
A. "Yes, sir, I *guess*. I didn't see him anymore."

Q. "Did Mr. Winchester leave money in the cash register when you cleaned up at night?"
A. "He don't leave much in it, I don't think. I never counted it."

Q. "Did you see him take the gun from the building at any time?"
A. "No."

Q. "Did Mr. Winchester say *anything* to you?"
A. "No."

Q. "When did you see Mr. Winchester again?"
A. "I haven't seen him anymore."

Q. "He never came back while you were working Mr. Bierbaum?"
A. "Not that I know of."

Q. "Who works nights at Club 37, Mr. Bierbaum"?
A. "Shot or Bill Harris."

Q. "Who came in to work the night shift April 7?"
A. "I told Bill Harris to take over."

Q. "What did you do when Bill Harris took over?"
A. "I ran to bed in the cabin."

Q. "Did Mr. Winchester live in Club 37?"
A. "Yes, he had a room in the back."

Q. "Did you see Mr. Winchester in his cabin?"
A. "His bedroom is in the back. I did not see him."

Q. "During the day, did you see anyone come in Club 37 and ask for Mr. Winchester or was looking for him?"
A. "Sheriff Aldridge and Investigator Clifford."

Q. "When was that"?
A. "That was on Friday morning, I believe, around 11:00 o'clock."

Q. "Did Mr. Winchester live in Club 37 or in the cabin?"

A. "He had his bedroom in the back of Club 37."

That ended the questioning of Otto Bierbaum.

Coroner Paul Baur called Bill Harris to the stand to testify.

Q. "I wish you'd state your name to the jury and where you live"
A. "Bill Harris. I live at #217, 7ᵗʰ Street in Cairo with my mother right now."

Q. "Where did you live Friday?"
A. "Club 37."

Q. "Where did you live there?'
A. "In the living quarters, over in the cabins."

Q. "Is that your regular job? Working for Mr. Winchester?"
A. "No, I'm a truck driver for Mr. Edgar Stephens Construction Co. I help Shot out sometimes."

Q. "Does your wife work for Mr. Winchester?"
A. "Yes, she worked pretty regularly."

Q. "Did you take the night shift Friday night?'
A. "Yes, sir, I did. Peggy, my wife was helping me."

Q. "Bill, did you see Mr. Winchester at any time after you began work or did you talk to him during your work shift?"

A. "Yes, I talked with Mr. Winchester around 2:30 or so but did not see him."

Q. "Where was Mr. Winchester at that time?"
A. "He was over in Peggy and my living quarters."

Q. "What time did you close the club up for the night?"
A. "Oh, I guess it was around 12:30 or 1:00 in the morning."

Q. "Tell the jury what you did from closing time until you were told that Mr. Winchester was mortally wounded."
A. "I closed up at 12:30 to 1:00 in the morning. I checked the register, put the amount of money on the slip of paper, counted the money in the drawers, put that on the slip of paper, and put the slip in the register. Closed the register and the building. I came to Cairo to talk with Mr. Clifford about quarter to 2 in the morning. Wasn't it around 2 Mr. Clifford?"

Mr. Clifford responded from his chair that it was 1:15 in the morning.

Bill Harris continues his testimony.

"I talked to Mr. Clifford about an hour then went back to Club 37, pulled up alongside our quarters and walked to the door. Winchester opened the door and said, "Bill, you all can't stay here tonight. Go over to the place and stay. And he gives me the keys to the place and I asked him what was the matter. I knew what the deal was and he said to me, "Well, I'm not going to jail." I asked him to just go and give yourself up and he said, "I'm not going to give myself up Bill, I'll shoot my head off before I give myself up. And he pulled this gun out.

Q. "When you speak of a gun, who did the gun belong to?"
A. "Well, I guess you could say it belonged to me."

Q. "Where did you buy the gun?"
A. "At Paducah, Kentucky."

Q. "What did you pay for your gun?"
A. "Mr. Winchester paid $27.50 for the gun."

Q. "Did you have it on you Friday night?"
A. "I had it inside the coat packet of the red/maroon jacket that Shot had on that night."

Q. "You were not wearing your maroon jacket the night you worked? Mr. Winchester was wearing *your jacket* that night?"
A. "Yes."

Q. "You did not take your gun to the club that night while you worked? But you bought the gun for protection while you worked your shift?"
A. "No. I did not take the gun with me to work."

There was stirring among the jurors after Bill Harris answered the question.

Q. "Go ahead and tell the jury what happened next."
A. "My wife and I were in Mr. Winchester's cabin sleeping. I did not hear anything until later in the morning. About 7:00. Mr. Aldrich came into the club and made a phone call. I hear him say they found Mr. Winchester and he had been shot. I jumped out of bed and went to where Mr. Aldrich was.

Q. "How did Sheriff Aldrich get into the club if you had locked it up the night before?"
A. "Otto Bierbaum had already opened up. I don't know why so early."

That ended the questioning of William Harris.

Coroner Baur called Carl Bode to testify.

Q. "Mr. Bode. The crime scene pictures I have here were taken by you correct?"
A. "Yes."

Q. "You were called up to the scene of the crime to take pictures *after* they took the body out of the car. Correct?'
A. "That's right."

Q. "Who took the picture of Mr. Winchester *still in the car?*"
No response from Carl Bode.

Q. "Mr. Bode, what time did you get there? At the scene?"
A. "I got there at the time Sheriff Aldrich was leaving Club

37 to go back to the scene of the shooting. There was he and I, Mr. Dennis and his son."

Q. "No police officials protecting the scene?"
A. "No sir."

Q. "Are you a professional photographer Mr. Bode?"
A. "Halfway. Half hobby, more or less."

That ended questioning of Carl Bode.

Paul Shelton was sworn in to testify by coroner Paul Baur.

Q. "Please tell the jury Mr. Shelton what your occupation is."
A. "I'm a truck driver."

Q. "On the morning of April 7th did you have occasion to be with your truck in the process of going around on old Route 37?"
A. "I was in my automobile."

Q. "Please tell the jury what you saw on the old Route 37."
A. "I left Olmsted about 4:30 that morning going south. I turned off new Route 37 and took the old Route 37. I was going about 30 miles per hour. I was going to pick up a friend. Just as you cross the concrete bridge behind the cylinder pile, I saw this car parked on the right, on his right, headed north on this road. So this car starts pulling out on the road with his lights off. I dimmed my lights and slowed down to about twenty. He kept coming and

meeting me with his lights off. He must have been driving ten or fifteen miles an hour. I rolled my window down on the driver's side and leaned out the window to get a better look at the car and driver. He never did turn his lights on. I could only see one man in the car. He was bareheaded, with his shirt collar unbuttoned and had a brown jacket on. I could tell the car was a '56 Oldsmobile. He still had his lights off after we passed. I went on to my friend's house, about 400 hundred yards from where I met this car and we got in this man's yard. My friend was out in the yard. I told my friend that I had just seen a man in a car pull out in the road with his lights off. And while we were there talking, this car came back headed south. He still had his lights off driving about 16 miles per hour. I asked my friend." What do you think he is up to?" My friend said, "If he is out with a married woman the light's going to catch him if he don't hurry up." The car then headed toward Mound City and we never saw the car anymore.

(There was laughter from the jury.)

Q. "Mr. Shelton, you couldn't recognize who was in the car?"
A. "No. His hair was reddish brown and he was slim, was all I could see."

Q. "Did you know Mr. Winchester?"
A. "I had met him on the road and had seen him from the highway around his place of business."

Q. "Who was the friend you were going down the road to

pick up?"

A. "Leslie Parker. He lives 350 or 400 yards from where I met the car. The car was headed north. I was headed south. Parker lives on the right hand side going south."

Q. "Where were you when you saw him the second time?"

A. "In Parker's yard, approximately 100 yards from the edge of the pavement and about 200 yards south of the pile of cinders where I saw the car pull out on the road."

Q. "Did you see who was driving from there?"

A. "When this car was going south, Parker was already in the yard putting his two dogs in the trunk of his car. I got my car and pulled it out in the road behind this other car but I never saw this other car again."

Q. "About what time was this?"

A. "About 5A.M. It was dark enough that we could only see one occupant."

That ended the questioning of Paul Shelton.

Leslie Parker was duly sworn in to testify for question asked by Coroner Paul Baur.

Q. "Mr. Parker, are you the man Paul Shelton, who just testified, went to see the morning of April 7th?"

A. "I'm the man the boy came to pick up. Yes sir."

Q. "Give the jury your full name and where you live."

A. "Leslie Parker and I live approximately two hundred yards south of where Mr. Winchester was found dead."

Q. "Mr. Parker, tell what you saw after you got into Mr. Shelton's car."
A. "I can't tell you anything after I got into the boy's car."

Q. "Didn't you see the car going south?"
A. "Yes sir. I was standing on the ground, putting the dogs in the truck. This boy came to the house and said he'd seen a man parked-he said, "who was the man in the two-tone Oldsmobile?" Before daylight, I saw a car pass my house two or three times. I opened the house door but couldn't see no one in the car. We were going to Marion to the dog race. We were putting these two beagle hounds in the car. We come out in the road and started south, but we never did see anybody no more."

Q. "Do you know Mr. Winchester?"
A. "Yes sir."

This ended the questioning of Leslie Parker.

Harlan Dennis was duly sworn in to testify to questions by Coroner Paul Bauer.

Q. "Please state your name and where you live.
A. "Harlan Dennis. I live out there at the old Clancy Tavern where the tavern burned."

Q. "Do you know Mr. Winchester?"
A. "Well, I've seen him a time or two. But I wasn't personally acquainted with him."

Q. "What time was you on old Route 37?"
A. "It was around 5:30, something like that. After I let my cow graze an hour or so.

Q. "Where do you live in relation to the cider pile that we spoke of?"
A. "I reckon 600 yards about it."

Q. "Tell the jury what you saw."
A. "I was taking my cow to pasture and saw this car sitting down there. It is nothing to see a car there most any time during the day or night. I stayed around with the cow a couple of hours. I seen that car over there with the door glass down. I thought I would go on ahead over to the car. I come down on the right and on my side of the road and I seen a man's feet laying over there on the car seat, and I went on and reported it. I called Sheriff Aldrich."

Q. "Was the car door open at that time?
A. "No sir. The driver's glass was rolled down."

Q. "Did you see anything unusual about the other door glass?"
A. "Only that there was a bullet hole through it."

Q. "Did you see anyone around the car or hear any shots?"
A. "No sir."

Q. "When you saw the car was it parked in front of the cinder pile?"
A. "He was coming from the south and out off the road and hit the sand pile."

(The jury mumbled between themselves. The crime photos showed the car facing south and head on into the cinder pile. Had the car been moved by someone after it was found after the Sheriff arrived on the scene? If so who moved it?)

Q. "He wasn't in front of the cinder pile?"
A. "No sir. He was in front of the *sand* pile and the motor was still running!"

Q. "You made no attempt to turn the engine off?"
A. "No sir."

Q. "Did you know who the person was?"
A. "No sir. When the sheriff got there I asked who it was."

Q. "Did you see the bullet hole in the right window?"
A. "Yes."

Q. "Did you notice a hole in the back window?"
A. "It was in the *rear* window behind the back seat in the right hand corner.

That ended the questioning of E.W. Dennis.

LaVera Mae Ford was duly sworn in to testify to questions by Coroner Paul Baur.

Q. "Would you tell the jury your name and where you live?"
A. "LaVera Mae Ford. I live at Urbandale.

(The day after Shot Winchester was killed Miss Ford moved out of the cabin to Urbandale.)

Q. "Where do you work?"
A. "I haven't been working."

Q. "Are the licenses of the Club 37 in your name?"
A. "Yes sir."

Q. "They are not in Mr. Winchester's name?"
A. "No sir."

Q. "Did you see Mr. Winchester Friday at any time?"
A. "No sir. The last time I saw Mr. Winchester was Wednesday night."

Q. "Did he tell you anything about that he might kill himself or anything like that?"
A. "No sir."

Q. "Have you ever heard that he has said something like that?"
A. "No sir."

Q. "Did you ever see him with a gun?"
A. "He didn't have or own a gun."

That ended the questioning of LaVera Mae Ford.

Cora 'Izzy" Winchester was duly sworn in to testify to Coroner Paul Baur's questions.

Q. "Please give your name, where you live, and your relationship to Lester Winchester."
A. "Cora Winchester. I now live in Rosiclare and I'm Lester's wife."

Q. "How long have you lived in Rosiclare?"
A. "I guess four or five years. Back and forth. I spent part of the time there at the club and part of the time with my family."

Q. "Did you see Lester 'Shot' any time after 7A.M. Friday morning?"
A. "Yes, I saw him at the place Friday night-Friday evening."

Q. "About what time was that?"
A. "Between 7:30 and 8:30."

Q. "Where were you when you talked with him?"
A. "Out in the living quarters in the cabin."

Q. "Did he tell you about the indictment?"

A. "Yes."

Q. "What did he tell you?"
A. "He told me that he had been indicted for murder on this murder charge."

Q. "Did he give you any money?"
A. "Yes, a large sum."

Q. "What else did he give you?"
A. "He gave me his diamond ring and told me to take care of them for his son."

Q. "How old is your son?"
A. "11 years old."

Q. "Did he tell you what he was going to do? Did he tell you that he was going to try and get him first?"
A. "He said he was not going to prison; that he would kill himself first."

Q. "Did you know he had a gun at that time?"
A. "I didn't see one."

Q. "Do you remember how he was dressed?"
A. "I couldn't see too well in there. It was dark. Light was coming from the bedroom but not enough to tell his clothing."

Q. "Did you try to prevail on him not to do it? If so what did he say?"

A. "Yes, I tried to get him to go back to Rosiclare with me. He said, "I've made up my mind. There is nothing you can do or say to stop me. He sensed that road blocks would be set up."

Q. "What did you do then and what time did you leave the cabin?"
A. "I left at 8:30 and went back to Rosiclare."

Q. "Did he ever say that to you before that night?"
A. "Yes, he was in prison as a boy and swore he would never go back to jail or prison again."

Q. "Did he ever talk to you about being in trouble in anyway?"
A. "Yes. He told me about the Reahm statement that got him indicted."

Q. "You knew he was indicted on some other stuff?"
A. "Yes."

That ended the questioning of Mrs. Winchester.

Sheriff Robert A. Aldrich was duly sworn in to testify to questions by Coroner Paul Baur.

Q. "Tell the jury your name and where you live?"
A. "Robert A. Aldrich and I live in Mound City."

Q. "Your profession is what?"

A. "County Sheriff of Pulaski County."

Q. "You had occasion to go out there after he had been shot?"
A. "Yes sir."

Q. "You also were on duty prior to that correct?"
A. "Yes."

Q. "Please tell the jury what you did beginning with Friday morning at 7:00 at the time that Mr. Winchester was in his place of business."
A. "About 8:00A.M., the Grand Jury was called and we took Alfred Reahm over before the Grand Jury. An indictment was returned between 11:00 and 12:00 against Lester Winchester for murder. This was due to Alfred Reahm naming Winchester as third person involved in the Adams murder. I then returned home and ate lunch. Then I and Frank Clifford went over to the Circuit Clerk's Office at about quarter to 1P.M. We picked up the bench warrant and went up to Club 37 where we talked to the bartender, Otto Bierbaum. He told us he hadn't seen Mr. Winchester since about 10A.M. that morning. Around 5:30, Clifford and I went back to Club 37 where we talked with Otto Bierbaum and Peggy Harris. They both said they hadn't seen him yet. While all of us were talking, Bill Harris came and we talked for a while and then Clifford and I went back to the County Jail. About 10:30P.M., we went back to Club 37 and we couldn't see his car anywhere. We went back to the jail and Mr. Clifford went home. Between 12:30 and 1 A.M.my, wife and I went back past Club 37 and the

car was still not there. We didn't go in. We drove up to Olmsted and come back to Mound City. At 6:00A.M. my wife and I again drove up past Club 37 and the car was not there and again we went back home. I was getting ready to take Alfred Reahm to the penitentiary when I got a call from Harlan Dennis saying that there was a car up on old Route 37 with a body in it. I immediately drove up there, looked in the car, and saw it was Lester Winchester. My radio in my car was out. I saw he was still breathing and I went to Club Winchester and called my wife and told her to call the ambulance, also to call Frank Gifford and my deputies. The motor was running and I did not shut it off until the ambulance got there. I think Carl Alstat reached in and turn the motor off. After removing Winchester we set up stakes and ropes around the car to keep anybody from touching it."

Q. "Did you notify the State Crime Department to come down and investigate and did they come?'
A. "Yes, sir. I did and they came."

Q. "They took the necessary finger prints from all over the car?"
A. "Yes."

Q. "You had removed the car to the Mound City Fire Department because of wind conditions?"
A. "Yes, sir."

Q. "When you say you went back and forth to Club 37, did you at any time go down old Route 37?"

A. "No, sir."

Q. "Always the *new* Route 37?"
A. "Friday night I went to Judge Reynolds' office to get the necessary papers signed on Alfred Reahm, and I talked to him in regard to Winchester, and he told me not to worry about it, the chances were he would come in Saturday morning with his attorney and his bondsman."

(Sheriff Aldrich never answered the question and it was not repeated. Why?)

Q. "Do you know whether he made an effort to get a bondsman during the night?"
A. "I've checked on it and can't find anybody that he talked to."

Q. "Before you removed the body or took the stuff out, did you see the gun any place?"
A. "Yes sir, the gun was lying on the floor board, underneath the steering wheel."

Q. "Was Mr. Winchester's right hand any way near the gun?"
A. "His right hand was hanging practically over the gun?"

Q. "Did you see a rag or towel in the front seat on the floor?'
A. "No sir, I did not."

Q. "Have you a letter from the State Crime Department?"

A. "Yes, sir. I have it with me. This is the one from Thomas E. Coleman who is a finger print technician, and he states in this letter that they had taken the prints. The letter says, "We do not have Winchester's prints on file in this Bureau. However, according to our information, Winchester was sentenced to Menard Penitentiary in 1913 on a murder charge and paroled August 4, 1924. Will check the latent prints found in the car with Winchester's when we receive a copy of his prints from Menard."

Q. "They took the necessary fingerprints from all over the car?
A. "Yes, sir."

Q. "You had removed the car to the Mound City Fire Department because of wind conditions?"
A. "Yes, sir."

Q. "And that's where they took the prints?"
A. "Yes, sir."

With this question and answer, the jury stirred once again fearing that the prints could have been smeared in the move."

Q. "In looking at the automobile, did you see any bullet holes?"
A. "Yes, there was one in the passenger door window, and one approximately in the middle of the back glass, behind the back seat."

Q. "How many shells were exploded in that revolver they

found in Mr. Winchester's car?"
A. "Three."

Q. "Where was the shot that was fatal?"
A. "It entered his head about his right ear on the right hand side."

Q. "In relation to the front seat of that car, in what position was Mr. Winchester?"
A. "He was laying right in the seat, with his head right against the left door."

Q. "That would make him move over to the opposite side of the car and fall under the steering wheel, correct?"
A. "Yes, sir. And that is where the blood was on the seat. The right hand seat."

Q. "Opposite the driver's seat?"
A. "Yes."

That ended the questioning of Sheriff Robert Aldrich.

Special Investigator, Frank Gifford was duly sworn in to testify to questions by Coroner Paul Baur.

Q. "Mr. Gifford where do you work?"
A. "For the city of Cairo.

Q. "Has the city of Cairo or the Sheriff's Department have an official photographer that they usually call?"

A. "Yes they do. The city of Cairo has Henry Moreland and the Sheriff of Pulaski County uses Mr. Carl Bode."

Q. "You were there when these photos were taken?"
A. "Yes, sir."

Q. "He was hired by the City of Cairo to take these pictures?"
A. "He was over at the hospital."

Q. "You saw him take these pictures?"
A. "Yes, sir."

Q. "Was the serial number ground off that gun?"
A. "Yes it was. An acid test was used on the gun and the numbers 6953 appeared. The rest was not identifiable. The gun that was bought in Paducah had those numbers recorded as sold to William Smith, which was the alias that Bill Harris used to purchase the gun.

Q. "Could the gun have been given to someone else to use?"
A. "Yes, I suppose it could have."

This ended the questioning of Investigator Frank Clifford.

Peggy Harris was duly sworn in to testify to questions by Coroner Paul Baur.

Q. "Mrs. Harris, where do you live?"

A. "At 217, 7th street in Cairo, Illinois."

Q. "Where did you live prior to Mr. Winchester's death?"
A. "On the premises around Club 37."

Q. "You worked for Mr. Winchester?"
A. "I did."

Q. "Did you work on Friday, April 7th and if so what hours?"
A. "Yes, I did. I worked from 7:30 or 8:00 o'clock?"

Q. "Where you with your husband, William, when the conversation was made about not coming in?"
A. "I was."

Q. "You heard everything that your husband said?"
A. "I did."

Q. "Did you see Mr. Winchester at any time that night?"
A. "No, sir."

Q. "Did you ever see a gun around the tavern itself, or in any of the drawers?"
A. "No, sir, I never did."

Q. "But you knew Bill owned this other gun?"
A. "No, sir."

Q. "You don't know when Mr. Winchester got hold of it at any time?"

A. "No, sir."

Q. "Did Mr. Winchester usually carry a lot of money on him?"
A. "I've seen Mr. Winchester pay bills when standing behind the bar and I've seen him make change."

Q. "Would you say he had a lot of money on his person like seven or eight hundred dollars?"
A. "He could have had all ones as far as I know, but he did carry money on him."

Q. "Did you ever see him with a purse or wallet?"
A. "No, sir, I never did."

Q. "What are your usual working hours and what do you do at the club?"
A. "I cook supper and someone always watches the bar. After supper, my husband and I or Mr. Winchester usually worked around in there.

This ended the questioning of Peggy Harris.

Jack Tallo was duly sworn in to testify to questions by Coroner Paul Baur.

Q. "State your name and where you live for the jury."
A. "Jack Tallo. I live at 217, 9ᵗʰ street in Cairo, Illinois."

Q. "Do you have a business in Cairo?'

A. "Yes, sir."

Q. "You knew Mr. Winchester?"
A. "Yes, sir."

Q. "Did he come into your business very much?"
A. "Quite often, yes."

Q. "He isn't the owner and he's not interested in your business?"
A. "No, sir."

Q. "And you have no interest in his business?"
A. "No, sir."

Q. "When was the last time he was in your business?"
A. "About a week before he killed himself."

Q. "Wasn't he in your place Friday night?"
A. "No, sir."

Q. "Wasn't you in his place?"
A. "No, sir."

Q. "Did you ever hear Winchester say anything about killing himself?'
A. "No, sir. Never."

Q. "Isn't your place of business outside Cairo's city limits?"
A. "You asked where I lived and I told you!"

Q. "Where *is* your place of business?"
A. "Future City, Illinois.

Q. "When Mr. Winchester was in your place of business, did you ever see him with what you would call a large amount of money?"
A. "No, sir."

Q. "Did he drink much, to your knowledge?"
A. "Very little, if any."

This concludes the inquest of Mr. Lester Winchester.

The jury was given instructions to take whatever time was needed to return with a ruling on Lester "Shot' Winchester's death. While sequestered in a jury room, the jury debated the many questions they had about the inquest. The overall feeling was that the inquest was not conducted correctly with several of the interviews.

On several occasions the jury was unsettled by responses given by those testifying. Their questions were:

1. Bill Harris had convinced Shot to go with him to purchase a gun 4 days before Shot was killed because he would feel more secure working at Club 37. However, Harris did not take the gun with him to work the night Shot was killed. His wife, Peggy was not even aware that there was a gun around.

2. Bill Harris testified that Shot was wearing *his* (Harris) jacket the night he was killed. Why? Shot had his own jacket. Was there a way to identify whose jacket was whose?

Why wasn't this asked of Harris? Could Harris prove that Shot was wearing Bill Harris' jacket?

3. The jurors felt that the witnesses appeared to have been told how to respond prior to testifying. Many of the questions ask of them by Coroner Paul Baur were leading which led the witness to know what to say as a response.

4. The crime scene photos taken caused great concern as the photographer, Carl Bode, stated he took the pictures before anyone had touched the body. Mr. E. W. Dennis, the man who *discovered* Winchester, testified that Winchester's feet were "on the car seat." Mr. Bode stated that they were on the car's floorboard. There was no cross examination to this dispute.

5. Sheriff Robert Aldrich testified that the car was removed to a fire department to take fingerprints. The possibility of smearing some prints was great and the official lab test results said, 'many were smeared'.

Sheriff Aldrich stated that Shot's right hand was 'practically hanging over the gun' that was on the car's floorboard. The crime photo clearly shows his left arm under his shoulder and his left hand resting on his left thigh. His right arm and hand laid over his right leg...nowhere near the gun.

Sheriff Aldrich testified that he had left police officers at the scene to secure the crime scene. Carl Bode testified that no one was present at the scene when he got there.

The jury at this point believed that the body was handled before some of the pictures were taken. Why wasn't the discrepancy questioned?

6. The most damning conflict in testimony was Mr. Dennis distinctly stated that the car was headed into the sand pile. Sheriff Aldrich said the car was headed into the cinder pile. Mr. Dennis was asked if he meant cinder pile and he emphatically stated *sand* twice. There were two different piles at the highway building. One pile was sand and further down was a pile of cinders. The two piles were of very different colors. The subject was immediately changed. Was the car, with the body in it, *moved* from the actual scene of the shooting before witnesses were around?

7. Two pictures of the crime scene show the gun in two different positions. This was not explained nor questioned.

8. The jury questioned the statement by Sheriff Aldrich that his radio *was out!* This was taken by the jurors as not working. The jury found that hard to believe.

9. That Aldrich testified his *wife* was with him on police business was another great concern to the jury. Was this a common police procedure?

10. There was concern among the jurors that Dr. Robinson had not been subpoenaed to testify. It had been stated that no gunshot residue was on Winchester's hand or clothing.

11. What happened to the bullet remains removed from Shot's head? Where were the other bullets? The crime lab results stated no positive proof that bullet found in victim came from gun found at scene.

They were interested in more facts about the autopsy but not granted a copy of the report. Why not?

12. Finally, Jack Tallo's testimony that Shot Winchester was in his place of business (a tavern) about a week "before he killed himself." Whether Shot had been killed or committed suicide had not *been* determined at that point. Yet Mr. Tallo was not corrected and the statement stood for the record. The jury felt that the witnesses were told to lean toward a suicide as a cause of death rather than present the evidence in an impartial way. There was just too much evidence that showed something very sinister about the crime.

When the Grand Jury convened again at the Alexander Court House in Cairo, Sheriff Aldrich was present for the verdict. Dan Sullivan, jury Foreman, read the findings.

"We, the jurors, recommend that the Sheriff and other officials of Pulaski County should make further investigations into Lester Winchester's death and report such findings to the State's Attorney of Pulaski County and also to the Grand Jury of Pulaski County, the county in which the incident was committed."

Hearing this Sheriff Robert Aldrich stormed out of the courthouse. He got into his car and immediately left the area. State Trooper Don Evers and area police officers were happy that the jury requested further investigations. They and others present at the inquest knew it wasn't a suicide.

The Lester Winchester case was *never* reopened! Pulaski County *never* re-investigated the crime. It was *never meant* to be re-opened. That would mean finding a suspect or suspects to a murder. It was important to end the case with an inquest verdict of suicide. Local law enforcement, judiciary personnel, and local politicians were all involved in the cover up. John D'Arco, a Chicago Alderman, made sure downstate judges were 'influenced' to downgrade charges of corruption from Effingham to Cairo and west to East St. Louis. The gun found in the car disappeared from evidence and showed up months later in a shoebox. Special Investigator Frank Gifford was in a position to insist on a re-investigation but never pursued the case. Was he threatened too? This is justice in southern Illinois.

Frank 'Buster' Wortman, Jake Rubin, and George and Art Garner were thugs. Hoods, criminals and killers that made no apology for pushing the legal business world aside and developing their own network of businesses sucking the innocent into the vacuum of this unpublished group.

Most of the area mobsters that lived by the gun died by the gun. Ben Fishel was murdered in 1960 by a Chicago team probably led by Marshall Califano of the Chicago Syndicate. Califano was muscle in the Chicago gambling racket. Local mobsters had planned to terminate Fishel the same night, but Chicago got to him first. No one was ever arrested. Jake Rubin was killed in his own club shortly after Fishel. George Garner was arrested for that murder. George Garner was later killed in a Missouri house fire he had been hired to set by a local judge. Frank 'Buster' Wortman died of cancer in 1968.

Shot Winchester and others like him fought against the criminal element in the area every day. Most of them lost in one way or another. The crimes they fought against were not due to some foreign entity but man-made. Little Egypt was the Garden of Eden for Illinois but became the breeding bed for evil. The lawlessness and violence in the southern counties, specifically Alexander and Pulaski Counties, in no way deserve celebration. The crimes in these southern counties didn't end with the Lester 'Shot' Winchester case. They continue to go on. New vices have replaced illegal gambling and bootlegging. New faces have taken over where Jake Rubin, Buster Wortman, and the Garner brothers once ruled. As long as there are those who want a piece of the action, whether legal or illegal, the new faces of the criminal element will be there... waiting for them.

The dishonor to the laws of the land by respected police officers and judges, the greed and open corruption of trusted politicians, and the tolerance of the same by the citizens may be said to be the greatest sin of all.

ABOUT THE AUTHOR

Maureen Hughes has made a career in investigating crime. She has a degree in Criminal Justice and has worked for the Chicago branch of the IYC and downstate police departments. *Sins of The South* is the second true crime book written by her. She has authored six titles in all. Raised in Illinois, she shares her time between properties in Illinois and Nevada.

58185282R00121

Made in the USA
Lexington, KY
04 December 2016